CU00828103

25

STUDY GUIDE

Britain: Health and the People, c1000 to the Present Day

AQA - GCSE

app
available

Published by Clever Lili Limited.

contact@cleverlili.com

First published 2020

ISBN 978-1-913887-24-7

Cover by: Original artwork by Leonardo DaVinci on Adobe Stock

Icons by: flaticon and freepik

Contributors: Hayleigh Snow, Muirin Gillespie-Gallery, Emily Bishop, Lynn Harkin, Marcus Pailing, Shahan Abu Shumel Haydar, James George

Edited by Paul Connolly and Rebecca Parsley

Design by Evgeni Veskov and Will Fox

DISCOVER MORE OF OUR GCSE HISTORY STUDY GUIDES

GCSEHistory.com and Clever Lili

Elizabethan England, c1568–1603

Conflict and Tension between East and West, 1945–1972

Germany, 1890–1945: Democracy and Dictatorship

America, 1920–1973: Opportunity and Inequality

Britain: Power and the People, c1170 to the Present Day

Norman England, c1066–c1100

Conflict and Tension: The First World War, 1894–1918

Russia, 1894–1945: Tsardom and Communism

America, 1840–1895: Expansion and Consolidation

Conflict and Tension: The Inter-War Years, 1918–1939

Britain: Migration, Empires and the People, c790 to the Present Day

Conflict and Tension in Asia, 1950–1975

Contents

Modern Medicine

In this study guide, you will see a series of icons, highlighted words and page references. The key below will help you quickly establish what these mean and where to go for more information.

Icons

? **WHAT** questions cover the key events and themes.

👤 **WHO** questions cover the key people involved.

⏳ **WHEN** questions cover the timings of key events.

📍 **WHERE** questions cover the locations of key moments.

🗲 **WHY** questions cover the reasons behind key events.

⚙ **HOW** questions take a closer look at the way in which events, situations and trends occur.

📌 **IMPORTANCE** questions take a closer look at the significance of events, situations, and recurrent trends and themes.

💡 **DECISIONS** questions take a closer look at choices made at events and situations during this era.

Highlighted words

Abdicate - occasionally, you will see certain words highlighted within an answer. This means that, if you need it, you'll find an explanation of the word or phrase in the glossary which starts on **page 102**.

Page references

Tudor *(p. 7)* - occasionally, a certain subject within an answer is covered in more depth on a different page. If you'd like to learn more about it, you can go directly to the page indicated.

Britain: Health and the people: c1000 to the present day, is a thematic study that looks at the change and continuity of medicine through British history. You look at the main people, events and developments, as well as the significant features of the different ages, from medieval to modern times.

Purpose

In studying this course you will be able to view the process of change and continuity across time and make comparisons between different ages. You will assess how different themes played a part to instigate or hold back changes. The course also draws on wider world developments that had an impact on these themes.

Key factors

Within each of the time periods the course looks at specific factors. These are:

- ☀ War.
- ☀ Superstition and religion.
- ☀ Chance.
- ☀ Government.
- ☀ Communication.
- ☀ Science and technology.
- ☀ The role of the individual.

Key timeperiods

The medicine through time course is split into time periods. Across which you will need to discuss the changes and continuities that occur. These time periods are:

- ☰ Medicine stands still - this focuses on the Middle Ages.
- ☰ The beginnings of change - this focuses on the Renaissance.
- ☰ A revolution in medicine - this focuses on the 18th and 19th centuries.
- ☰ Modern medicine - this focuses on the 20th century and present day.

Assessment

Britain: Health and the people: c1000 to the present day, is assessed in Paper 2, and is worth 25% of your overall grade.

Questions

The exam paper on Britain: Health and the people: c1000 to the present day contains a total of four questions:

- ❓ Question 1 is worth 8 marks. This question will require you to examine a SOURCE, and assesses your ability to analyse and evaluate how useful the source is using your contextual knowledge to support or challenge what is shown.

- ❓ Question 2 is worth 8 marks. This question will require you to explain the significance of a different theme, person or event by using your contextual knowledge and looking at the consequences. To analyse significance you need to look at their immediate impact, the impact over time and the impact today.

- ❓ Question 3 is worth 8 marks. This question will require you to identify two similarities between two different events, discoveries or people. This will give you the opportunity to show your ability to explain and analyse using 2nd order concepts such as similarity and difference.

- ❓ Question 4 is worth 16 marks plus 4 marks for spelling, punctuation and grammar. Here you will be required to make a judgement about the role of a certain factor throughout medicine.

Revision! A dreaded word. Everyone knows it's coming, everyone knows how much it helps with your exam performance, and everyone struggles to get started! We know you want to do the best you can in your GCSEs, but schools aren't always clear on the best way to revise. This can leave students wondering:

- ✔ How should I plan my revision time?
- ✔ How can I beat procrastination?
- ✔ What methods should I use? Flash cards? Re-reading my notes? Highlighting?

Luckily, you no longer need to guess at the answers. Education researchers have looked at all the available revision studies, and the jury is in. They've come up with some key pointers on the best ways to revise, as well as some thoughts on popular revision methods that aren't so helpful. The next few pages will help you understand what we know about the best revision methods.

How can I beat procrastination?

This is an age-old question, and it applies to adults as well! Have a look at our top three tips below.

◎ Reward yourself

When we think a task we have to do is going to be boring, hard or uncomfortable, we often put if off and do something more 'fun' instead. But we often don't really enjoy the 'fun' activity because we feel guilty about avoiding what we should be doing. Instead, get your work done and promise yourself a reward after you complete it. Whatever treat you choose will seem all the sweeter, and you'll feel proud for doing something you found difficult. Just do it!

◎ Just do it!

We tend to procrastinate when we think the task we have to do is going to be difficult or dull. The funny thing is, the most uncomfortable part is usually making ourselves sit down and start it in the first place. Once you begin, it's usually not nearly as bad as you anticipated.

◎ Pomodoro technique

The pomodoro technique helps you trick your brain by telling it you only have to focus for a short time. Set a timer for 20 minutes and focus that whole period on your revision. Turn off your phone, clear your desk, and work. At the end of the 20 minutes, you get to take a break for five. Then, do another 20 minutes. You'll usually find your rhythm and it becomes easier to carry on because it's only for a short, defined chunk of time.

Spaced practice

We tend to arrange our revision into big blocks. For example, you might tell yourself: "This week I'll do all my revision for the Cold War, then next week I'll do the Medicine Through Time unit."

This is called **massed practice**, because all revision for a single topic is done as one big mass.

But there's a better way! Try **spaced practice** instead. Instead of putting all revision sessions for one topic into a single block, space them out. See the example below for how it works.

This means planning ahead, rather than leaving revision to the last minute - but the evidence strongly suggests it's worth it. You'll remember much more from your revision if you use **spaced practice** rather than organising it into big blocks. Whichever method you choose, though, remember to reward yourself with breaks.

Spaced practice (more effective):

week 1	week 2	week 3	week 4
Topic 1	Topic 1	Topic 1	Topic 1
Topic 2	Topic 2	Topic 2	Topic 2
Topic 3	Topic 3	Topic 3	Topic 3
Topic 4	Topic 4	Topic 4	Topic 4

Massed practice (less effective)

week 1	week 2	week 3	week 4
Topic 1	Topic 2	Topic 3	Topic 4

What methods should I use to revise?

Self-testing/flash cards

Self explanation/mind-mapping

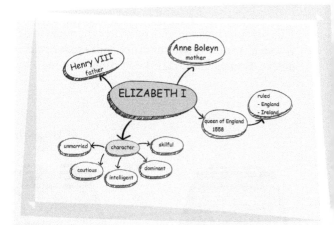

The research shows a clear winner for revision methods - **self-testing**. A good way to do this is with **flash cards.** Flash cards are really useful for helping you recall short – but important – pieces of information, like names and dates.

Side A - question

Side B - answer

Write questions on one side of the cards, and the answers on the back. This makes answering the questions and then testing yourself easy. Put all the cards you get right in a pile to one side, and only repeat the test with the ones you got wrong - this will force you to work on your weaker areas.

pile with right answers

pile with wrong answers

As this book has a quiz question structure itself, you can use it for this technique.

Another good revision method is **self-explanation**. This is where you explain how and why one piece of information from your course linked with another piece.

This can be done with **mind-maps**, where you draw the links and then write explanations for how they connect. For example, President Truman is connected with anti-communism because of the Truman Doctrine.

Quizzes, amazing exam preparation tools and more at GCSEHistory.com

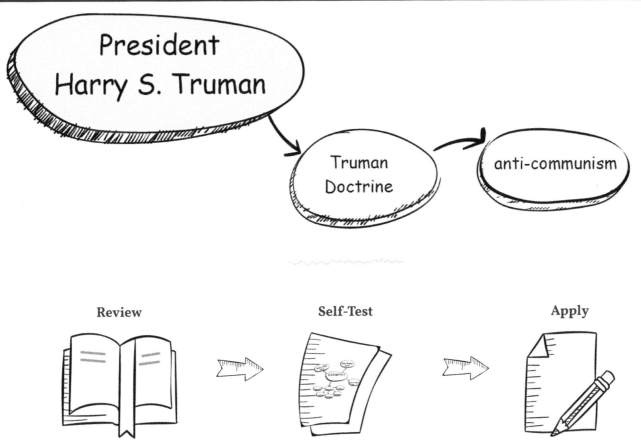

Review	Self-Test	Apply
Start by highlighting or re-reading to create your flashcards for self-testing.	Test yourself with flash cards. Make mind maps to explain the concepts.	Apply your knowledge on practice exam questions.

 Which revision techniques should I be cautious about?

Highlighting and **re-reading** are not necessarily bad strategies - but the research does say they're less effective than flash cards and mind-maps.

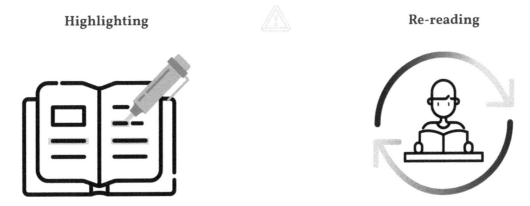

If you do use these methods, make sure they are **the first step to creating flash cards**. Really engage with the material as you go, rather than switching to autopilot.

TIMELINE

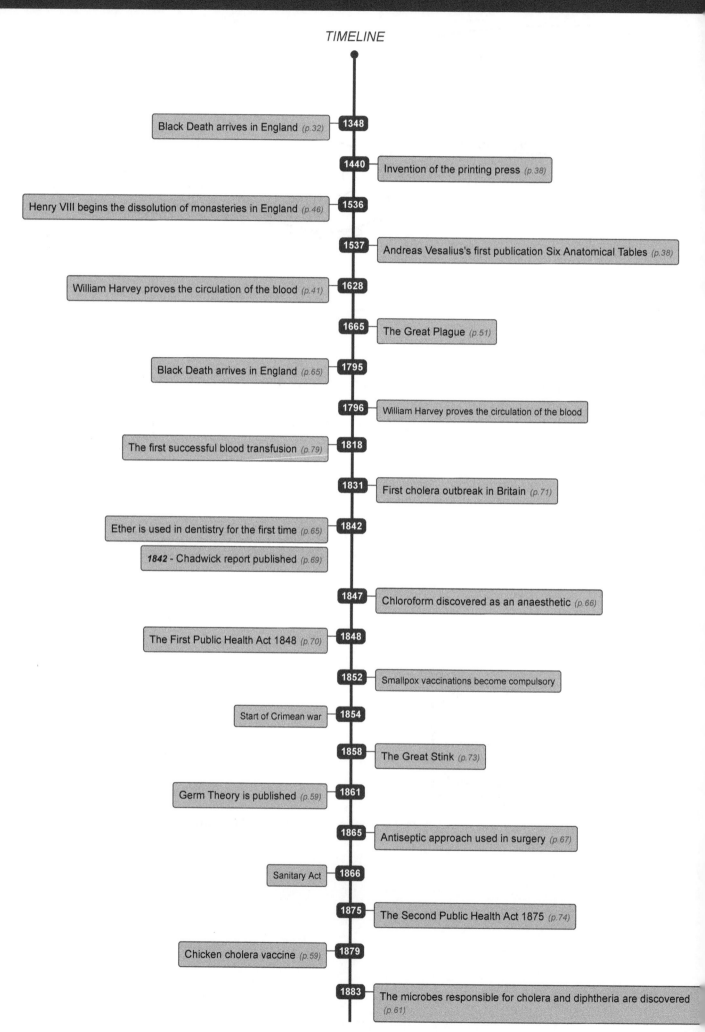

Black Death arrives in England *(p.32)* — **1348**

1440 — Invention of the printing press *(p.38)*

Henry VIII begins the dissolution of monasteries in England *(p.46)* — **1536**

1537 — Andreas Vesalius's first publication Six Anatomical Tables *(p.38)*

William Harvey proves the circulation of the blood *(p.41)* — **1628**

1665 — The Great Plague *(p.51)*

Black Death arrives in England *(p.65)* — **1795**

1796 — William Harvey proves the circulation of the blood

The first successful blood transfusion *(p.79)* — **1818**

1831 — First cholera outbreak in Britain *(p.71)*

Ether is used in dentistry for the first time *(p.65)* — **1842**

1842 - Chadwick report published *(p.69)*

1847 — Chloroform discovered as an anaesthetic *(p.66)*

The First Public Health Act 1848 *(p.70)* — **1848**

1852 — Smallpox vaccinations become compulsory

Start of Crimean war — **1854**

1858 — The Great Stink *(p.73)*

Germ Theory is published *(p.59)* — **1861**

1865 — Antiseptic approach used in surgery *(p.67)*

Sanitary Act — **1866**

1875 — The Second Public Health Act 1875 *(p.74)*

Chicken cholera vaccine *(p.59)* — **1879**

1883 — The microbes responsible for cholera and diphtheria are discovered *(p.61)*

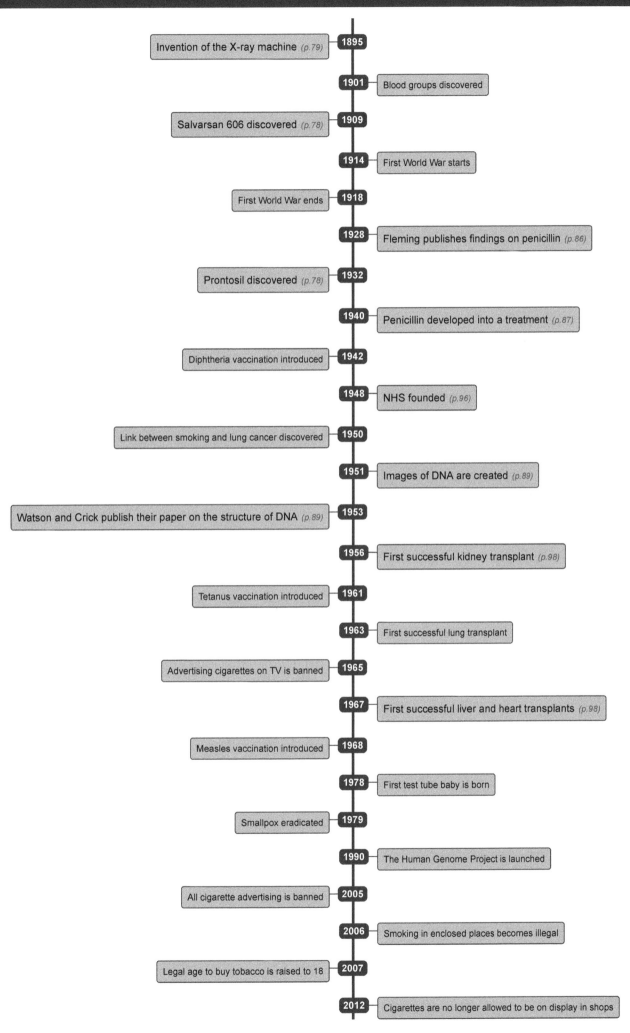

Invention of the X-ray machine *(p.79)* — **1895**

1901 — Blood groups discovered

Salvarsan 606 discovered *(p.78)* — **1909**

1914 — First World War starts

First World War ends — **1918**

1928 — Fleming publishes findings on penicillin *(p.86)*

Prontosil discovered *(p.78)* — **1932**

1940 — Penicillin developed into a treatment *(p.87)*

Diphtheria vaccination introduced — **1942**

1948 — NHS founded *(p.96)*

Link between smoking and lung cancer discovered — **1950**

1951 — Images of DNA are created *(p.89)*

Watson and Crick publish their paper on the structure of DNA *(p.89)* — **1953**

1956 — First successful kidney transplant *(p.98)*

Tetanus vaccination introduced — **1961**

1963 — First successful lung transplant

Advertising cigarettes on TV is banned — **1965**

1967 — First successful liver and heart transplants *(p.98)*

Measles vaccination introduced — **1968**

1978 — First test tube baby is born

Smallpox eradicated — **1979**

1990 — The Human Genome Project is launched

All cigarette advertising is banned — **2005**

2006 — Smoking in enclosed places becomes illegal

Legal age to buy tobacco is raised to 18 — **2007**

2012 — Cigarettes are no longer allowed to be on display in shops

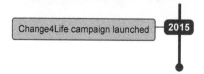

Change4Life campaign launched — 2015

BRITAIN: HEALTH AND THE PEOPLE

MEDIEVAL BELIEFS: CAUSES OF DISEASE

A time when faith was everything

 What were medieval beliefs about disease?

The causes of disease were a mystery. People believed supernatural *(p.16)* causes could lead to illness.

DID YOU KNOW?

Medieval psychiatry was brutal!
A treatment given to the mentally ill included tying up the patient's legs and arms, and then putting their feet into salt war while pulling their hair and nose and squeezing their toes and fingers tightly!

SUPERSTITIOUS BELIEFS

One of the explanations for ill health in the Middle Ages was supernatural causes

 What supernatural explanations did people hold about health?

People in medieval England often relied on superstition when it came to health. They believed in supernatural explanations for health and disease.

 What were the most common supernatural explanations of causes of disease in the medieval period?

There were 4 main supernatural elements believed to cause disease.

- ☑ Many believed that diseases were the will of God. The Catholic Church taught that, if someone committed a sin, God would punish them with sickness.
- ☑ People believed that illness was a test of faith.
- ☑ Some people believed that supernatural demons could inhabit people's bodies and cause illnesses.
- ☑ Witches were thought to be responsible for spreading diseases.
- ☑ Some people thought astrology was to blame - that the way the stars and planets were aligned could cause disease.

 Why did people have supernatural explanations about the causes of disease?

Religion was a major force in medieval England, and the Catholic Church had a lot of influence over people's lives. Ther was also a lack of scientific knowledge. This led to people believing in supernatural reasons for disease and sickness.

 What were the main supernatural beliefs for treatment of disease in medieval medicine?

There were three main treatments for diseases based on superstitious beliefs.

- ☑ Prayers were said to ask God's forgiveness. The rich could pay for prayers to be said on their behalf. Many people used flagellation (whipping themselves).
- ☑ People went on pilgrimages to important religious shrines or tombs.
- ☑ Physicians used horoscopes to treat patients. They would consider two dates: the patient's date of birth and the date their illness began. They would use this information to work out how to treat them.

Quizzes, amazing exam preparation tools and more at GCSEHistory.com

RATIONAL BELIEFS

Ideas about what caused disease in the middle ages could also be rational

Were there any rational explanations for why people got sick?

Not all ideas about the causes of disease were based on supernatural *(p.16)* beliefs. Some were based on rational explanations.

What were the rational explanations for the causes of disease?

People believed two main rational explanations for the causes of disease.

- ☑ Miasma theory was the idea that bad air from dead bodies, rotting food, or other organic matter caused disease.
- ☑ Another idea was the illness was caused by an imbalance of the 'four humours' within the body - blood, yellow bile (choler), black bile and phlegm.

HIPPOCRATES

Known as the 'Father of Medicine'

Who was Hippocrates?

Hippocrates was an ancient Greek physician. He believed in observing a patient's symptoms, and treating them using natural treatments.

What were Hippocrates' ideas?

There are three main theories attributed to Hippocrates.

- ☑ Clinical observation, which says a doctor should examine and monitor a patient's symptoms to diagnose their illness. Treatments should be based on these observations.

- ✅ The Hippocratic Oath, which was taken by physicians. It was a promise to follow a set of ethical standards to treat their patients well and to cause no harm.
- ✅ The Theory of the Four Humours, which says that a person needed balanced humours in order to be healthy. People got diseases if they had too much or too little of any humour *(p. 18)*.

DID YOU KNOW?

The Hippocratic Oath written by Hippocrates is still held sacred by physicians.

Although many physicians do not swear to the original oath, swearing a modified form of the Hippocratic Oath remains a rite of passage for medical graduates in many countries.

MEDIEVAL CAUSES OF DISEASE - FOUR HUMOURS

Hippocrates' theory of the four humours states that the human body is made up of four substances

What was the humours theory?

The Theory of the Four Humours stated that, to be healthy, a person needed to have balanced humours. People would get diseases if they had too much or too little of any humour.

What were the humours according to the Theory of the Four Humours?

There were four humours.

- ✅ Choler, or yellow bile, was considered hot and dry, and related to summer and fire.
- ✅ Blood was hot and wet, and related to spring and air.
- ✅ Phlegm was cold and wet, and related to winter and water.
- ✅ Black bile was considered cold and dry, and was related to autumn and earth.

How did doctors balance yellow bile according to the Theory of the Four Humours?

To balance yellow bile (choler), doctors would purge patients, by making them vomit or by changing their diet.

How did doctors balance blood according to the Theory of the Four Humours?

Bloodletting was used to balance blood. This was most often done by barber surgeons or wise women.

How did doctors balance phlegm according to the Theory of the Four Humours?

To balance phlegm, doctors recommended breathing steam or eating vegetables filled with water.

How did doctors balance black bile according to the Theory of the Four Humours?

Doctors gave their patients laxatives and suggested they eat more vegetables to balance black bile.

How did Galen of Pergamon add to the Theory of the Four Humours?

Galen *(p. 19)* built on the Theory of Four Humours by adding the Theory of Opposites for treating an imbalance. For example, he taught that too much blood (a fever) could be cured by cool things, such as eating cucumber.

Why was the Theory of the Four Humours important?

There are three main reasons why the Theory of the Four Humours was important.

- ☑ It became the basis for how patients were treated for more than 1,400 years.
- ☑ It appeared to include all illnesses. Therefore, in order to apply the theory, physicians would deliberately manipulate what they observed to fit it.
- ☑ There was a lack of scientific knowledge at that time which stopped people challenging the theory or providing alternative treatments.

DID YOU KNOW?

Each 'humour' was also linked to an element.

Each of the four 'humours' was linked to an element. Blood was matched with air, phlegm with water, yellow bile with fire and black bile with the earth.

GALEN

Galen was a Roman physician, philosopher and writer of Greek origin.

Who was Claudius Galen?

Claudius Galen was an ancient Roman physician, surgeon and writer of Greek origin. He was the personal surgeon to the Roman Empire Marcus Aurelius, and wrote over 350 books.

What were Galen's scientific beliefs?

Galen believed in the Theory of the Four Humours and built on it by developing the Theory of Opposites. He supported clinical observation, and encouraged doctors to monitor a patient's pulse or take a urine sample to determine what was wrong.

Why did the Christian Church support Galen?

Galen said that the human body must have been designed because it fit together so well. This supported the Church's teachings that God created humans.

What were Galen's theories?

There were two main theories associated with Galen.

- ☑ Galen based his Theory of Opposites on the Theory of the Four Humours. He taught that illnesses could be cured by using treatments that opposed a patient's symptoms. For example, if there was an excess of blood - which was considered hot and wet, and could lead to illnesses such as a fever - then the treatment should be cold and dry.
- ☑ Galen supported the miasma theory, which was the belief that disease was caused by bad air.

What mistakes did Galen make?

Galen had carried out some dissections on animals, as human dissection was forbidden by the Church. This meant he made some mistakes.

- ☑ He believed that the jaw was made up of two bones.
- ☑ He did not understand about blood circulation, and thought that blood was made in the liver, then absorbed by the body, rather than being pumped around it.

☑ He said that men had one fewer pair of ribs than women.

Why were Galen's ideas supported for so long?

Galen's ideas were significant for 2 main reasons:

☑ Galen's ideas had the support of the Church. Its influence over peoples' beliefs ensured his ideas were followed as the foundation of medicine for 1,400 years.

☑ There were a lack of alternatives to his ideas and little opportunity to question them.

Why were Galen's books important?

Galen's books were important because many people could not read, so any doctor who had read them was considered very intelligent.

What made Galen hard to challenge?

There was a lack of scientific evidence to challenge what Galen taught, because the Church would not allow human dissection.

DID YOU KNOW?

Galen was just 13 when he wrote his first book!

Three Commentaries on the Syllogistic Works of Chrysippus' was the first known book produced by Galen when he was just thirteen years old!

MEDIEVAL PREVENTION

There were four main ways in which people tried to prevent disease in the Middle Ages.

How did people try to prevent illness in medieval times?

There were four main methods of prevention used in medieval times: religion, purifying the air, diet, and the regimen sanitatis.

How did the medieval Church try to prevent illness?

The most important ways were trying to not commit any sins, praying regularly and paying tithes to the Church.

How did people try to prevent miasma in medieval times?

People tried to purify the air to protect themselves from miasma. Local councils put measures in place to make sure the streets were cleaned.

How did people use diet to prevent illness in medieval times?

People believed if you ate too much it could cause an imbalance of humours, so people often used to purge themselves as a way to treat this.

How did physicians try to prevent illness in medieval times?

Physicians would write instructions, called the regimen sanitatis, for healthy living. It was only used by the rich as it was very expensive: it would instruct them to take baths and make sure their houses were clean.

Quizzes, amazing exam preparation tools and more at GCSEHistory.com

---

DID YOU KNOW?

People ate emeralds to prevent the Black Death!
It was thought that eating crushed minerals, such as emeralds, would keep the Black Death away.

MEDIEVAL TREATMENT

The cures and treatments used in the Middle Ages were a mixture of religion, superstition and herbal remedies.

What was medieval treatment like?

Medieval treatment *(p.33)* was very limited as it was mostly based on the supposed superstitious and religious causes of disease. It was also sometimes inaccurate due to a lack of medical knowledge and understanding.

What treatment was available for most medieval people?

There were 5 main ways in which you could get treatment:

- ☑ Rich people would consult a physician.
- ☑ There were hospitals, but people went to them for rest and prayer rather than medical intervention.
- ☑ Most people were cared for in the home by the women in their family.
- ☑ People could visit barber-surgeons to have simple surgical procedures.
- ☑ Apothecaries provided medicinal treatments using plants and herbs.

Why did women give medieval treatment in the home?

It cost money to see a physician and most people could not afford it.

How did medieval women give treatment at home?

Women used treatments that they learned from other women in their household. They would mix remedies using herbs from their gardens and do their best to make their patients comfortable. Women also acted as midwives at births.

What was the religious approach to treatment in medieval times?

As people believed that God created illnesses as a punishment for sinning, then the treatment involved a religious act such as fasting, paying for a special mass, prayer, or pilgrimage.

What was the supernatural approach to treatment in medieval times?

Using charms or chanting spells was believed to scare off illness and heal people. Astrology was also used, as physicians referred to star charts to determine when certain treatments could be carried out.

What was the humoural approach to treatment in medieval times?

Bloodletting, purging and the Theory of Opposites were used to help balance the humours.

What was the remedial approach to treatment in medieval times?

Herbal remedies were inhaled or drunk to treat illnesses. Sometimes bathing in water with flowers and herbs was encouraged as it was believed it could help balance the humours by removing blockages.

 ### Where could the poor go for treatment in medieval England?

The poor could be treated by women in their home. They could also seek rest in a medieval hospital *(p.22)*; but, although they would be made comfortable there, they would not receive medical treatment.

DID YOU KNOW?

Salt was very precious!

Salt was a very precious resource in the Middle Ages and was believed to have a medicinal purpose. If salt was spilt, it was no longer allowed to be used for medicine and was then gathered up and thrown over the left shoulder so that it would blind the evil spirits that people believed constantly followed them around.

HOSPITALS

Providing health care, shelter and hospitality

 ### What were medieval hospitals like?

In medieval times, hospitals were mostly run by the Church, with monks and nuns to care for patients.

 ### How were people cared for in medieval hospitals?

Hospitals were focused on caring for patients, not curing them. Monks and nuns kept patients comfortable, and made sure their beds faced the hospital's altar.

 ### Who did medieval hospitals look after?

Hospitals cared for different types of people in medieval times.

- ☑ Hospitals for lepers were set up. These hospitals were not inside towns, but were on the outskirts, as lepers were considered outcasts.
- ☑ Medieval hospitals were also used to house the poor and elderly.
- ☑ Hospitals that did care for the infirm only provided basic nursing.

DID YOU KNOW?

47% of medieval hospitals were almshouses, which cared for the poor and the destitute.

PHYSICIANS

Hospitals then weren't anything like contemporary hospitals.

What were medieval doctors prohibited from doing?

Physicians who were monks were not permitted to dissect dead bodies or carry out treatment that would involve cutting a patient. This led to bloodletting and other surgeries being carried out by barber surgeons.

What training did medieval doctors have?

Medical training was arduous, with a medical degree taking seven to ten years to complete. Potential doctors studied the works of Hippocrates *(p. 17)* and Galen *(p. 19)*. Very few had the chance to dissect a body. As there weren't many physicians, seeing one cost a lot of money.

What was the role of the medieval Church in training doctors?

Many universities were funded by the Catholic Church, which meant their teaching was influenced by the Church's beliefs.

What methods did medieval doctors use?

Medieval physicians used 4 main treatment methods:

- ☑ Diagnosis. Medieval physicians rarely treated patients themselves. Instead they would carry out a diagnosis and recommend a course of treatment to be carried out by a barber surgeon *(p.24)* or an apothecary. *(p.23)*
- ☑ Sample study. Physicians would study their patients' blood, urine and faeces to reach a diagnosis.
- ☑ Astrology. Physicians would look at astrological charts to see how the stars were aligned when their patient was born and when they fell ill.
- ☑ Study of 'humoural *(p.18)* tendencies'. These were personality traits believed to be linked to your humours. For example, a quick-tempered person was believed to have too much yellow bile.

Why did not many people visit a medieval physician?

Most doctors were based in large towns, and even so there weren't many of them. Consulting them was expensive, so most people could not afford to see them.

DID YOU KNOW?

The first hospital in England was in the 1070s!

Following the Norman Conquest, the earliest hospital known in the UK was founded in Harbledown near Canterbury in the 1070s.

APOTHECARIES

The person who mixed herbal remedies

What were apothecaries?

Apothecaries were people who sold herbal remedies. They had good knowledge of the healing powers of plants and herbs.

How did apothecaries train?

Apothecaries were not trained at university, instead they gained most of their knowledge from family members and through experience. Many also used a book called 'Materia Medica' to study herbal remedies.

Who visited apothecaries?

As many people were too poor to see a physician, they would visit an apothecary instead as their services were much cheaper. As a result, apothecaries were viewed as rivals to their businesses by physicians.

DID YOU KNOW?

Unlike physicians, apothecaries did not take the Hippocratic Oath.

This meant that they were not bound by the instruction to do no harm, and might mix poisons if they were asked to do so.

BARBER SURGEONS

Barber surgeons had no formal training but could perform surgical procedures

---

What were barber surgeons?

Barber surgeons were barbers who had no formal university training. They had access to sharp blades so performed some medical procedures, such as pulling teeth, and bleeding patients to treat some illnesses.

What medical procedures did barber surgeons perform?

Barber surgeons would usually carry out the following surgeries:

- ☑ They would pull teeth.
- ☑ They also performed minor surgeries and, in some cases, even amputations.
- ☑ Bloodletting.

What were the risks in using a barber-surgeon?

A lot of people died because their wounds became infected. Barber surgeons also often over-bled their patients which resulted in death.

DID YOU KNOW?

Barbers are one of the oldest professions in the world!

There are paintings from Ancient Egyptian tombs that show a barber cutting hair, and also relics of razors found which are nearly 6,000 years old.

Quizzes, amazing exam preparation tools and more at GCSEHistory.com

MEDIEVAL SURGERY

Very, very slow progress

? What was surgery like during medieval times?

Surgery in medieval times was backwards, dangerous and very few patients survived.

What were the problems with surgery in medieval times?

There were 3 main problems with surgery in medieval times:

- ☑ Pain: the pain was excruciating and there were no real anaesthetics. Natural anaesthetics like hemlock or opium were used to numb pain, but they were dangerous as a high doses could kill the patient. The pain could be so bad that some patients died of shock.
- ☑ Infection: because there was no understanding of what caused them, many patients died from post-surgery infections. Many doctors believed that the presence of pus in wounds helped patients recover. Dirty surgical instruments were seen as a sign of a surgeon's experience.
- ☑ Blood loss: blood transfusions did not exist and patients often lost a lot of blood during surgery, which could be fatal.

Who made progress in surgery during the medieval period?

There were a number of doctors who helped with the progression of surgery during medieval times:

- ☑ John Arderne *(p.25)*.
- ☑ Abulcasis.
- ☑ Hugh and Theodoric of Lucca *(p.26)*.

DID YOU KNOW?

Physicians began to be commonly known as 'doctors' in the 16th century.

The word 'doctor' was initially used in the 13th century by the universities of Bologna and Paris to describe people with medical training who were qualified to teach others.

JOHN ARDERNE

A father of surgery

👤 Who was John Arderne?

John Arderne was an English surgeon.

What were John Arderne's achievements?

John Arderne had 3 key achievements:

- ☑ In 1376, he wrote a book called Practica which is known for its realistic drawings of surgical instruments and operations.
- ☑ He managed to invent workable cures and would charge knights a fee to treat their anal abscesses.
- ☑ He helped establish the Guild of Surgeons in 1368.

HUGH AND THEODORIC OF LUCCA

Father and son

Who were Hugh and Theodoric of Lucca?

Hugh and Theodoric of Lucca were father and son. They were both Italian surgeons.

What were Hugh and Theodoric of Lucca's achievements?

Hugh and Theodoric of Lucca had 3 main achievements:

- ☑ In 1267, they wrote a book that contradicted the belief that pus was needed to heal wounds.
- ☑ To reduce the probability of infection, they advocated pouring wine onto wounds.
- ☑ They developed a method and used new tools to extract arrows from a body.

CHRISTIANITY - HELP OR HINDRANCE?

In the Middle Ages, the Catholic Church established monasteries which were also hospitals. They also provided training for doctors.

What were Christian ideas about medieval medicine?

Christians believed that they should care for the sick because Jesus healed those who were sick. However, they also believed that illnesses were a challenge or punishment from God.

Why did medieval Christians treat their patients?

Because illnesses were seen as a possible punishment from God, Christians believed in caring for their patients, not curing them.

How did Christians treat their patients in medieval times?

Christians tried to treat people in 3 main ways:

- ☑ They would encourage people to pray to God.
- ☑ They would encourage people to go on a pilgrimage to visit a shrine of a holy person where they would be miraculously healed.
- ☑ The Christian Church financed many of the 700 hospitals in England between 1000 and 1500. Here, people could recover in tidy and quiet surroundings.

What were Christian hospitals like in medieval England?

Medieval Christian hospitals were characterised in the following 4 key ways:

- ☑ They provided care not cures.
- ☑ They varied in size from small hospitals that could accommodate 12 patients, which reflected the number of Jesus' disciples, to ones that could house 200 patients.
- ☑ Hospitals were attached to monasteries and were run by monks and nuns.
- ☑ Medieval hospitals often didn't have any doctors, but they would have a chaplain or a priest.

How did Christianity help progress medicine in medieval times?

Christianity helped medicine progress in medieval times in 4 main ways:

- ☑ Christians believed they had a duty of care which led to them help set up hospitals.
- ☑ They provided a place for some sick people to get treated.
- ☑ The Church established universities throughout Europe where people could study medicine using the books of Galen *(p.19)* and Hippocrates *(p.17)*.
- ☑ Monks would translate old medical texts - many arriving from the Islamic world.

How did Christianity hinder medical progress in medieval times?

Christianity hindered medical progress in medieval times in 4 key ways:

- ☑ The Church made dissection illegal, making it harder to learn about anatomy.
- ☑ The Church supported the ideas of Galen *(p.19)*, even though his work was based on dissections of animals. This made his ideas hard to challenge.
- ☑ Those who went against the ideas of Galen *(p.19)* and the Church could be arrested, like Roger Bacon in 1277.
- ☑ Some hospitals during this time would refuse to take in very sick people or women.

DID YOU KNOW?

Faith even influenced bed sizes!

Many hospitals had a capacity of twelve as this was reflective of the biblical twelve disciples. They could, however, be much larger.

ISLAMIC MEDICINE

Islamic medicine built on the principles set by Roman and Greek physicians such as Galen and Hippocrates.

What was Islamic medicine like?

Islamic medicine was more advanced than European medicine in medieval times.

Where was Islamic medicine developed?

The Islamic Empire was a single state ruled by a caliph. It included countries like Egypt, Persia and Arabia.

Why was Islamic medicine advanced?

There were 2 main reasons why Islam supported medical progress:

- ☑ Medical learning was promoted in Islam as the Prophet Muhammad had said that 'For every disease, Allah has given a cure'.
- ☑ As a result, the caliphs supported the development of medical knowledge and understanding as well as science.

How did caliphs help with the progression of Islamic medicine?

The caliphs helped Islamic medicine progress in 3 main ways:

- ☑ Baghdad developed into a key location where medical manuscripts were translated from Greek into Arabic under the rule of Caliph Harun al-Rashid.
- ☑ Many ancient Greek medical books were preserved in the Caliph Harun al-Rashid's library. The Dark Ages meant that these books were not available in Western Europe.
- ☑ The library became a place of learning for scholars because Caliph al-Mamun established the library as 'The House of Wisdom'.

What were Islamic ideas on health and medicine?

Islamic beliefs surrounding medicine were very different to Christian beliefs in the following 3 main ways:

- ☑ They had hospitals set up for people with mental illnesses where patients were treated with kindness rather than someone who was being punished by God.
- ☑ Islamic hospitals focused on treating people, unlike Christian hospitals that focused on caring for patients. For example, a new hospital with a library and medical school was established in Baghdad in 805 so that patients could be treated and cured.
- ☑ Treatment was provided for all people by building 'bimaristans' - hospitals located in many Islamic towns. Patients were treated regardless of their religion, gender or wealth.

Name some people who were important in Islamic medicine.

There were two key Islamic doctors:

- ☑ Al-Razi *(p.29)*.
- ☑ Ibn Sina *(p.29)*.

What was surgery like in Islamic medicine?

Muslims made 3 key important advances in surgery:

- ☑ They used cannabis and opium as anaesthetics.
- ☑ They used vinegar, mercury and alcohol as antiseptics.
- ☑ Al-Zahrawi *(p.30)* wrote a book on surgery which was the first medical book to include pictures of surgical equipment, many of which he invented, and how to use them. This book was widely translated throughout Europe.

DID YOU KNOW?

Islamic medicine was up to 300 years ahead of the west!

300 years before it was discovered in the West, Ibn Nafis, an Islamic polymath, wrote about blood circulating in the body in the13th century.

AL-RAZI

Al-Razi was a Muslim philosopher and alchemist.

Who was Al-Razi?

Al-Razi was a Persian physician and scholar in medieval times.

Who was Al-Razi known as in Europe?

Al-Razi was also known as Rhazes in western Europe.

What were Al-Razi's achievements?

During his time Al-Razi achieved many things. The 3 most notable are:

- ☑ He identified the differences between measles and smallpox.
- ☑ He taught that patients should be carefully observed in order to track symptoms.
- ☑ He wrote over 150 books - one of these was called 'Doubts about Galen' *(p.19)*.

DID YOU KNOW?

He didn't study medicine until he was in his thirties!

Before becoming one of the greatest physicians of the medieval period, writing over 200 works of which half were on medicine, Al-Razi was a musician and a money-changer.

IBN SINA

Mostly known in the West as Avicenna, Ibn Sina was a Persian polymath who is thought of as the father of early modern medicine.

Who was Ibn Sina?

Ibn Sina was a Persian physician.

Who was Ibn Sina known as in Europe?

Ibn Sina was known as Avicenna in Western Europe.

What were Ibn Sina's achievements?

During his time Ibn Sina achieved many things. The 4 most notable are:

- ☑ He wrote the 'Canon of Medicine', an encyclopedia containing all the medical knowledge and understanding of the Islamic and Greek worlds at that time.
- ☑ He knew of, and wrote about, the uses and properties of 760 drugs.
- ☑ He wrote about medical problems such as strokes, dealing with fractures and obesity.
- ☑ His book was very influential because it became the key medical text used by European medical schools and universities until the 1600s.

AL-ZAHRAWI

Al-Zahrawi is known as the 'father of surgery'

Who was Al-Zahrawi?

Al-Zahrawi was an Arab physician.

Who was Al-Zahrawi known as in Europe?

In western Europe, Al-Zahrawi was also known as Abulcasis.

What were Al-Zahrawi's achievements?

During his time Al-Zahrawi achieved many things. The 3 most notable are:

- ☑ He wrote a book called 'Method of Medicine'. It comprised 30 volumes and included medical data from over his 50 year career.
- ☑ He made around 200 detailed drawings of different surgical devices, many he had invented, and how to use them.
- ☑ He fully described how to perform certain advanced surgeries, such as craniotomies and tonsillectomies.

MEDIEVAL PUBLIC HEALTH

First steps taken

What was public health like in medieval times?

Public health in medieval times was a lot worse than it is today. However, the health and cleanliness of the people depended on whether you were living in a town or in a monastery.

Why was public health bad in medieval times?

People didn't have an understanding of the connection between germs and their link to disease and infection.

What was public health like in medieval towns?

Public health in towns was generally bad due to 5 key reasons:

- ☑ Many people used the rivers near towns to remove their waste and sewage. This is also where some people got their water from.
- ☑ Sometimes people would throw their waste onto the streets.
- ☑ There were privies with cesspits located beneath them in many towns and some houses. They would be annually cleaned by gong farmers; however the waste could pollute any nearby river if the cesspits were over-filled or overflowed.
- ☑ If there was a lot of rain the cesspits might overflow onto the streets.
- ☑ The streets in the poorer areas of towns would smell because they were dirtied by human and animal waste.

What was public health like for wealthy people in medieval towns?

Wealthier people generally had better public health for 3 main reasons:

- ☑ They could afford to have the areas around their house cleaned by servants.
- ☑ Some may have been lucky to be near an elaborate water supply system built by the Romans.
- ☑ They were more likely to have their own privies.

How was public health in medieval towns improved?

Public health in medieval towns was improved to a certain extent in 4 main ways:

- ☑ There were restrictions, put in place by some local craft guilds, on where certain businesses could operate. This is because some businesses, like leather tanneries and butchers, produced hazardous waste which they disposed of in nearby rivers which polluted the water.
- ☑ In 1371, the slaughter of large animals inside the walls of London was banned by the mayor.
- ☑ in 1388, a law was passed by Parliament which fined people £20 for throwing waste into ponds and rivers.
- ☑ In 1466, a law was passed in Worcester that stated that the entrails and blood of butchered animals had to be carried away the same day.
- ☑ In 1421, the Mayor of Coventry issued a proclamation that on every Saturday, everyone was responsible for cleaning in front of their house or they would be fined 12p.

What was public health like in a medieval monastery?

Public health in monasteries was better than that in towns.

Why was public health better in a medieval monastery?

Conditions in monasteries were better because:

- ☑ They were isolated.
- ☑ They were located near rivers.
- ☑ Fresh water was piped to the washing facilities in the monasteries.
- ☑ They had filtration systems that removed dirt from water.
- ☑ They had lavatoriums which were facilities for washing.
- ☑ Their privies were regularly emptied and the waste used as manure.
- ☑ It was possible to use local river water to 'flush' out the privies and cesspits in some monasteries.
- ☑ Monks believed that cleanliness is next to godliness, and that being clean was a sign of spirituality.
- ☑ Monks were instructed to have baths - sometimes every month or twice a year at Easter and Christmas.
- ☑ Twice a week, the monks would wash their feet, heads and faces in a religious ceremony.
- ☑ They had infirmaries.

Why did monasteries have better public health than towns?

Monasteries were able to have better public health conditions than towns for 6 key reasons:

- ☑ People paid money and gave land to these institutions in return for prayers and forgiveness from sins which made monasteries very wealthy.
- ☑ A considerable amount of profit was created from the production of wool by monasteries.
- ☑ Monasteries had extensive libraries containing medical books and therefore the monks were knowledgeable about medicine and health.
- ☑ Monks were disciplined and would follow the strict rules and routines of the monasteries.
- ☑ They had better health facilities, such as access to water, medicines, and infirmaries, compared to towns.
- ☑ They were were less exposed to diseases or epidemics, like the plague, because of their isolated locations.

DID YOU KNOW?

First steps to deal with unsanitary conditions of the cities

In this era, quarantine was introduced to help spread disease, the first hospitals appeared, and some medical and social care became available

---

BLACK DEATH

Catastrophe strikes in 1348

What was the Black Death?

The Black Death was an epidemic that hit England. It was the bubonic plague, a serious infection of the lymphatic system which caused buboes (pus-filled swellings) in the groin and armpits. People died within five days of becoming il

---

When did the Black Death arrive in England?

The Black Death arrived in England in 1348.

What did people think caused the Black Death?

People during the medieval period, people believed in 3 main causes of the Black Death:

- ☑ People thought it was caused by God, punishing people on earth for their sins.
- ☑ Some believed it was due to miasma (bad air).
- ☑ Astrologists blamed an unusual alignment of the planets in 1345, three years earlier.

How did the Black Death spread?

Bubonic plague was caused by bacteria in fleas' stomachs. Infected fleas were carried on the backs of rats to new places and then passed it to humans. The disease spread quickly because people lived close to each other at that time.

What did people do to stop themselves catching the Black Death?

People used 4 key methods to treat the Black Death.

- ☑ They prayed for God's forgiveness. Many carried out flagellation (whipping) to show they were sorry. Many believed the Black Death was God's will, so there was no way to cure it.

- ✅ Carrying strong-smelling herbs to ward off miasma was recommended by physicians. It was also believed that lighting fires and boiling vinegar would also have the same effect.
- ✅ Apothecaries created herbal remedies to try and treat the disease. Many were mixtures that had to be applied directly to the buboes.
- ✅ Some recommended lancing the buboes to release the pus.

What measures were taken to stop the spread of the Black Death?

People tried to prevent the spread of the Black Death and stop themselves catching it in 4 main ways.

- ✅ Some towns built cemeteries away from people's homes, because they believed the dead bodies caused miasma that was infecting people.
- ✅ Towns tried to ban travellers from entering. Local governments introduced quarantine laws stating newcomers must spend 40 days apart from any other people. They also considered banning large gatherings such as church services.
- ✅ Street cleaning was stopped by some local governments because they believed the smell from rubbish and waste would drive away the miasma.
- ✅ People went on pilgrimages, prayed, fasted, and whipped themselves to show God they were sorry for their sins. They hoped God would forgive them and not strike them down with the Black Death.

What was the impact of the Black Death?

The Black Death had a lasting impact on England for the following 5 main reasons:

- ✅ It is estimated the Black Death killed around a third of the population of England.
- ✅ The shortage of labourers meant that peasants could travel to where conditions and pay were better.
- ✅ The balance of power shifted towards the poorest in society, as feudalism came to an end.
- ✅ People began to challenge the social hierarchy. As the rich and wealthy were not immune from the disease, they were therefore not seen as better than others.
- ✅ The Church was also not immune from the disease, as many clergymen died.

When did the Black Death end?

The worst of the Black Death was over by 1350. It returned many times over the following decades, but infected fewer people each time.

DID YOU KNOW?

The bacteria responsible for the Black Death is called Yersinia Pestis.

CHANGE AND CONTINUITY IN MEDIEVAL MEDICINE

A time when medicine stood still

How did medieval medicine change over time?

Medieval medicine changed little due to religious and superstitious beliefs. Overall, the medieval period hindered medical progress.

What were the main changes to medicine in the medieval period?

There were 2 main aspects of change for medicine during the medieval period.

☑ By the end of the period, there were some hospitals and a few doctors who would treat poor people.

☑ Although they did not do it regularly, governments started playing a role in public health, through ordering places to be cleaned.

What stayed the same for medicine during the medieval period?

There were 5 main aspects of continuity for medicine during the medieval period.

☑ In order to treat everyday illnesses most people still depended on the work of local healers and women in the home.

☑ Most people still used herbal remedies to cure diseases.

☑ People still believed in the Theory of the Four Humours, as the Church's influence was so strong nobody challenged ideas it supported or accepted.

☑ Surgery was limited as there were no effective anaesthetics. The most frequent surgeries performed were tooth extractions, bloodletting and amputations.

☑ Religion still played an important role in explaining why people got sick.

DID YOU KNOW?

Snails were used to help with burns.
Using a live snail and rubbing it against the burn was one of many bizarre cures.

THE ROLE OF THE INDIVIDUAL IN MEDIEVAL MEDICINE

The individual played an important role in the development of medicine.

What role did individuals play in medicine in the Middle Ages?

There were a number of individuals who made discoveries and helped progress within medicine and surgery, although their overall impact varied.

What role did individuals play in medicine in the Middle Ages?

Here are some examples of the role that the individual played:

☑ John Arderne *(p.25)* developed a pain killing ointment for surgery, and had a high success rate for removing abcesses around the anus. His methods were outlined in his book 'The Practice of Surgery'.

☑ Muslim doctors al-Razi *(p.29)* and Ibn Sina *(p.29)* challenged the work of Galen *(p.19)*, which resulted in their views spreading to Europe.

THE ROLE OF SCIENCE AND TECHNOLOGY IN MEDIEVAL MEDICINE

Science and technology played an important role in the development of medicine.

What role did science and technology play in medicine in the Middle Ages?

Science and technology allow for new discoveries, and if utilised properly can result in lives saved. However, science and technology wasn't advanced in the Middle Ages so had little effect on the development of medicine.

What are some examples of science and technology influencing medicine in the Middle Ages?

Here are 2 main examples of the role that the science and technology played:

- ☑ Roman water supply systems had fallen into ruin, so some new towns used pipes made of poisonous lead.
- ☑ People didn't understand contagious diseases, which meant that the Black Death *(p.32)* spread quickly in overcrowded towns.

THE ROLE OF THE GOVERNMENT IN MEDIEVAL MEDICINE

The government played an important role in the development of medicine, however during the medieval period the government did not play a massive role.

What role did the government play in medicine in the Middle Ages?

Government had the ability to pass laws to improve public health. However, most attempts were made at a local rather than national level therefore limiting what could be achieved.

What are some examples of the government influencing medicine in the Middle Ages?

Here are 3 main examples of the role that the government played:

- ☑ In order to prevent the spread of the Black Death *(p.32)* in the mid-1300s, some local councils tried to quarantine infected places.
- ☑ Specialist hospitals were set up, such as St Bartholomew's in 1123 for pregnant women.
- ☑ Towns tried to stop businesses, like butchers, from polluting rivers.

THE ROLE OF COMMUNICATION IN MEDIEVAL MEDICINE

Communication played an important role in the development of medicine

What role did communication play in medicine in the Middle Ages?

Communication in the Middle Ages was difficult due to poor transport links, a lack of technology e.g. printing, and low literacy, so ideas about medicine spread slowly. Overall communication had a limited impact on the development of medicine.

What are some examples of communication influencing medicine in the Middle Ages?

Here are 3 main examples of the role that communication played:

- ☑ The works of Islamic doctors were translated and communicated to Europe through trade.

☑ Conditions were much better in monasteries because they had access to medical knowledge in books and people were more likely to be literate.

☑ Ibn Sina's *(p.29)* book Canon of Medicine was printed in Europe over 60 times in the 1500s.

THE ROLE OF RELIGION IN MEDIEVAL MEDICINE

Religion played an important role in the development of medicine and was probably the most important factor in medieval times

What role did religion and superstition play in medicine in the Middle Ages?

Religion and superstition were probably the most significant influences on health and medicine in the Middle Ages. While religion did help it progress in some ways, overall they had a stagnating effect.

What are some examples of religion influencing medicine in the Middle Ages?

Here are 3 main examples of the role that religion played:

☑ The Church controlled the universities, hospitals and the production of books.

☑ Health was better at Christian monasteries as they were isolated but were still near to rivers.

☑ The Church supported the ideas of Galen *(p.19)*, which were mistaken, and wouldn't allow anyone to challenge these beliefs, thereby hindering progress.

THE ROLE OF WAR IN MEDIEVAL MEDICINE

War played an important role in the development of medicine

What role did war play in medicine in the Middle Ages?

War played an important role in the development of medicine and surgery in the Middle Ages, as warfare provided the opportunity for people to gain experience working on the wounded.

What are some examples of war influencing medicine in the Middle Ages?

Here are 2 main examples of the role that war played:

☑ Wartime surgeons discovered the use of opium as a painkiller.

☑ John of Arderne's surgical textbook was based on his time in the Hundred Years War.

RENAISSANCE

A period where many old ideas were disproved, while new ones were being formed all the time

What was the Renaissance?

Meaning 'rebirth', it was time of great artistic and scientific progress. It was a period of transition from the ancient to the modern world.

When was Renaissance?

The Renaissance has no set dates but but it is generally considered to be around 1400 - 1600 in northern Europe.

What were some of the main developments during the Renaissance?

There are 3 key consequences of the Renaissance:

✅ Gunpowder was discovered which made wars and battles more bloody and led to new types of wounds.

✅ The idea of humanism was developed. This is the belief that high levels of human potential could be achieved through education.

✅ Global exploration led to the discovery of new lands and cultures, and therefore new medicines.

What changed in medicine during the Renaissance?

Changes to people's attitudes and ways of thinking during the Renaissance also led to 5 main changes in medicine.

✅ The Theory of the Four Humours fell out of favour with physicians as they began to understand that disease was something separate from the body, not caused by a person's humours being out of balance.

✅ A much greater understanding of anatomy developed. Doctors were able to carry out more human dissections as the power of the Church declined, which meant they could correct assumptions and mistakes made by Galen *(p. 19)* and others.

✅ Physicians no longer diagnosed patients from urine samples, and astrology also became less popular among medical professionals.

✅ Physicians came to rely more on their own observations, studies, and procedures such as dissections. They no longer relied on obtaining knowledge from books written by Galen *(p. 19)* and other doctors, although these were still used to research symptoms.

✅ Most of the medical advances were in the field of anatomical study, not treatment or prevention.

In what ways did medicine not develop during the Renaissance?

Although the Renaissance was a time of great change there were 3 main aspects of medicine which stayed the same:

✅ Ordinary people still held the same beliefs as their medieval ancestors about what caused illness. The Church remained a powerful force among the poor, so many still believed sickness was a punishment from God.

✅ Ordinary people continued to rely on the same treatments for disease as their medieval ancestors, including the need to balance the four humours, and the part played by religion.

✅ Miasma theory remained. Both physicians and ordinary people continued to believe disease could be caused by bad air. This was because there was no alternative explanation at the time.

How did medical training improve during the Renaissance?

During the Renaissance, there were 3 key improvements in medical training.

✅ Although physicians continued to learn from books, they were taught some new ideas about anatomy and chemistry.

✅ Surgeons had to obtain a licence and were now allowed to perform dissections.

✅ Apothecaries were also now licensed to trade, and had more ingredients and recipes from around the world.

DID YOU KNOW?

Soap wasn't readily available in the Renaissance.

Only really rich people could afford expensive olive oil soap. Most soap was made of animal fat and good for laundry, but too harsh for skin.

PRINTING PRESS

A technological change that impacted on the spread of medical ideas

What was the printing press?

The printing press is a machine used to reproduce writing and images. It uses ink on paper to make many identical copies.

When was the printing press invented?

The first printing press was created around 1440, through early experiments in printing. A commercial machine was available by 1450.

Who invented the printing press?

Johannes Gutenberg, a German goldsmith, is usually credited as the inventor of the printing press.

What was the significance of the printing press?

New ideas and medical knowledge could be spread more quickly due to the invention of the printing press.

Why was the printing press important for medicine?

There were 4 main reasons why the printing press was important in medicine.

- ☑ Publishing lots of copies of a theory meant many people had the chance to understand a theory in detail, and either object to or agree with it.
- ☑ Medical students were able to use books and manuals to help them learn.
- ☑ Books no longer had to be copied out by hand in monasteries, or only produced in Latin. It meant scientists could share information easily with each other.
- ☑ Control over what was published, and therefore which ideas influenced society, was no longer in the hands of the Church. This meant that the influence of Galen's *(p. 19)* ideas was reduced.

DID YOU KNOW?

The printing press made the written word quicker to produce, but also cheaper and more affordable.

ANDREAS VESALIUS

The father of modern anatomy

Who was Vesalius?

Andreas Vesalius was a Belgian physician. He trained at the universities of Louvain, Paris and Padua.

How did Vesalius make new discoveries?

Vesalius made many discoveries through dissection and by recording his discoveries in anatomical drawings. He stole bodies from cemeteries and gallows to dissect them, as well as dissecting the corpses of criminals.

What did Vesalius discover?

He identified approximately 300 mistakes in Galen's *(p.19)* work, including that:

- ☑ The human jawbone is formed from a single part, not two.
- ☑ Women do not have one more pair of ribs than men do.
- ☑ The human breast bone does not have 7 parts; it has 3 parts.

Why was Vesalius controversial?

Vesalius used dissections to show how Galen's *(p.19)* understanding of the human body was incorrect. This subsequently lost Vesalius his job at the university.

What was Vesalius's famous book?

Vesalius is most famous because of his book 'On the Fabric of the Human Body' which was published in 1543. The drawings of human anatomy in the book were exceptionally detailed.

Why was Vesalius significant?

Vesalius was very important for Renaissance *(p.36)* medicine for 4 main reasons.

- ☑ His work encouraged other doctors to question the old medical books and to learn through first-hand experience by performing dissections.
- ☑ His studies of the circulatory system were an important contribution to the understanding that the heart acts as a pump.
- ☑ The illustrations in 'On the Fabric of the Human Body' were copied and inserted into other books.
- ☑ Others were able to develop his work into the human anatomy further, because he provided the detailed ground work.

How was Vesalius's work brought to England?

Vesalius's work was transformed into a new book by Thomas Geminus called the 'Compendiosa'. All of his illustrations were copied and paired with surgical knowledge. This book became popular in England and was used by barber-surgeons.

DID YOU KNOW?

In the original Latin, Vesalius'ss book was called 'De Humani Corporis Fabrica Libri Septem'.

AMBROISE PARE

A war-time surgeon who made a chance discovery

Who was Ambroise Paré?

Ambroise Paré was a French physician who is regarded as the 'father of modern surgery'.

How were gunshot wounds treated in Paré's time?

In Paré's time, guns were relatively new inventions. People believed gunshot wounds were poisonous and used to treat them with hot oil, which they believed helped them heal.

What did Paré observe?

Paré observed that using hot oil on the wound was very painful.

 ### How did Paré improve the treatment of gunshot wounds?

During a French battle in 1537, Paré had to improvise when the hot oil ran out. Instead, he used a mixture of rose oil, egg white and turpentine to soothe his patients' wounds. Despite his worries, the patients slept well and their wounds healed quickly.

 ### How did Paré prevent patients bleeding to death during amputations?

Paré used ligatures, or string, instead of cauterisation during amputations. Cauterisation involved putting a red-hot iron on the wound from the limb's amputation. Paré used an older method to stop bleeding, by tying ligatures around individual blood vessels.

 ### Were problems did Paré encounter with his use of ligatures?

Ligatures could sometimes introduce infection to a wound because using them took longer than cauterising. Speed was crucial during battle.

 ### How did Paré help amputees?

Paré had to carry out a large number of amputations and quickly moved on to creating false limbs for wounded soldiers.

 ### What was the significance of Paré?

Paré had 2 main impacts on surgery during the Renaissance *(p.36)*:

- ✅ He translated some of Vesalius's work from Latin into French, working to increase surgeons' understanding of anatomy.
- ✅ His book, 'Works on Surgery', was circulated throughout Europe.

 ### How did Paré's work become popular in England?

Paré's work became popular in England for 2 key reasons:

- ✅ In 1591, an English version of his book was given to the library of barber-surgeons. It was printed for distribution in 1634.
- ✅ A number of English surgeons, most notably William Clowes, followed his approach to surgery.

DID YOU KNOW?

He was a royal surgeon!

During his career Pare was a surgeon to four French kings: Henry II, Francis II, Charles IX and Henry III.

WILLIAM HARVEY

Identifying the circulation of the blood

Who was William Harvey?

William Harvey was an English doctor who studied medicine at university in Cambridge and Padua. He specialised in physiology, and was physician to both James I and Charles I in England.

How did Harvey challenge the work of Galen?

He challenged Galen's *(p.19)* understanding that blood was made in the liver and that it was used as fuel. Harvey believed blood circulated around the body. This marked the beginning of the end of Galen's superiority.

How did Harvey explain blood circulation?

Harvey demonstrated how the heart was a pump for moving blood around the body. He used valves from a dissected heart to demonstrate that blood could only flow in one direction.

What were the limitations of Harvey's understanding of blood circulation?

Harvey's understanding of blood circulation was limited in 2 main ways.

- ☑ He did not understand why blood needed to circulate around the body.
- ☑ He did not know why blood in the arteries was different from blood in the veins.

Why did Harvey face resistance from other doctors?

Harvey made a major discovery, but the medical community was resistant to change for 3 key reasons.

- ☑ Blood transfusions to combat blood loss were now attempted, as Harvey's work demonstrated that this was essential. These attempts failed because there was a lack of understanding of blood groups. Therefore, his work was seen as not having much practical application.
- ☑ After so many years of Church dominance, during which Galen's *(p.19)* theories ruled medical understanding, people were reluctant to accept alternative information.
- ☑ As Harvey did not know why blood needed to circulate, or why the blood in arteries and veins was different, some other doctors rejected his ideas.

What was the significance of Harvey's work?

His theory of circulation was the first step towards blood transfusions becoming possible, and therefore saving lives. He was also one of the first to question Galen *(p.19)*. However, his impact at the time was small.

Which factors contributed to Harvey's discovery?

There were 4 main factors that helped Harvey's discovery.

- ☑ As an individual, Harvey was skilled, and was employed by Charles I. This gave him credibility and popularity.
- ☑ Institutions such as the Church were declining in popularity and influence, which meant that more people were challenging Galen's *(p.19)* work.
- ☑ Harvey was inspired by new technology, such as the mechanical water pump.
- ☑ Attitudes in society were changing. People were seeking scientific explanations during the Renaissance *(p.36)*. This influenced medicine in terms of people's understanding of the body, and the diagnosis and treatment of illness.

How did people react to Harvey's discovery?

People reacted to Harvey's discovery in 4 main ways.

- ☑ Some criticised Harvey and said that he was mad to suggest that blood circulated in the body.

- ☑ His ideas went against Galen (p.19), and some doctors refused to support him as a result.
- ☑ French anatomist Jean Riolan called Harvey a 'circulator', which meant that he was a 'quack'.
- ☑ Although some opposed him, his theory was accepted by many during his life.

DID YOU KNOW?

Harvey struggled to find acceptance for his theories.

They caused a loss of reputation and his business dropped as a result. He himself later called them his 'crackpot ideas'.

RENAISSANCE PREVENTION

The same ideas, but more government interference

What were the methods of preventing disease during the Renaissance?

There were 6 main methods of prevention in the Renaissance period. These were religion, purifying the air, fasting, remedies from apothecaries, some government public health actions, and equipment for doctors (such as outfits to help combat the Plague).

How did people believe religion prevented illness during the Renaissance?

People were advised to pray to God and repent their sins.

How did people prevent miasma during the Renaissance?

People were advised to purify the air by carrying a pomander. This was a ball of sweet smelling herbs.

How was diet used to prevent illness during the Renaissance?

Fasting was advised, as well as garlic-heavy diets.

What did apothecaries do to prevent illness during the Renaissance?

Apothecaries provided herbal remedies such as chewing dry tobacco to ward off the miasma.

How did the government try to prevent illness during the Renaissance?

The government played a much bigger role in public health, through quarantine laws and street cleaning.

How did plague doctors try to prevent illness during the Renaissance?

Plague doctors wore special beak-shaped masks, and coated their coats in wax so that blood and pus did not stick to it.

DID YOU KNOW?

Henry VIII closed down public baths - called 'stewes' - during his reign.

They were believed to cause the spread of syphilis or 'the Great Pox'. However, as syphilis is an STD and stewes were often used as brothels, there may have been some truth in this.

Quizzes, amazing exam preparation tools and more at GCSEHistory.com

EDWARD JENNER AND VACCINATION

Jenner was known as the father of immunology.

Who was Edward Jenner?

Edward Jenner was a country doctor who discovered vaccines.

What was Jenner known as?

Jenner was also known as 'the Father of Immunology'.

What was used before Jenner created vaccinations?

Inoculation involved spreading the pus from an infected wound into a cut on the skin of a healthy person. They would then catch a mild case of the disease and build up immunity.

What disease did Jenner help cure?

In the 18th century, smallpox was a big killer. It was highly infectious and spread from one person to another through coughing, sneezing or touching. It killed about 30% of the people who caught it.

What did Jenner observe?

In the 1790s, Jenner realised that milkmaids did not catch smallpox if they had already had cowpox.

What was Jenner's experiment?

Jenner's experiment involved deliberately infecting a boy with cowpox, then later infecting him with smallpox. The boy didn't catch smallpox as he had built up resistance to it.

Why was vaccination safer than inoculation according to Jenner?

Vaccination against smallpox proved that you didn't need to catch a disease directly in order to build up immunity to it. Jenner simply used a similar and milder disease, cowpox, to help protect against smallpox.

When did Jenner publish his theory on vaccination?

Jenner published his theory in 1798.

Why did Jenner call his discovery vaccination?

The name vaccine comes from the Latin word vacca, which means cow.

Why did Jenner face opposition to his discovery?

There were 6 main reasons Jenner faced opposition.

- ☑ The Church did not believe cows should play a part in healing humans, seeing it as unnatural.
- ☑ Inoculation doctors were angry, because inoculation was an expensive treatment that made them a lot of money. Vaccination would take away this income.
- ☑ Jenner was not well known in London, as he was a country doctor. As a result, many were reluctant to believe his findings. The Royal Society *(p.48)* refused to publish them.
- ☑ Dr William Woodville was in dispute with Jenner after some of his patients died from smallpox while using Jenner's techniques. However, Woodville's equipment was later shown to be contaminated.
- ☑ Jenner published his findings, but could not explain how vaccination worked. This made it difficult for other doctors to accept his theory.

☑ This discovery was made before germ theory *(p.59)*, so Jenner couldn't explain the link between cowpox and smallpox or reproduce the link with any other diseases.

Why was Jenner significant?

Jenner was significant for 2 main reasons:

☑ His smallpox vaccine was the first successful vaccine to be developed and led to the science of immunology.

☑ In 1852, the vaccine was made compulsory and in 1980, the World Health Organisation declared that smallpox had been eradicated.

DID YOU KNOW?

When he was young Jenner collected birds' eggs and fossils.

Recognising this love of natural history, his brother, Stephen, encouraged Edward to train as a surgeon.

RENAISSANCE TREATMENT

New ideas slowly make an impact

 ## Did treatments in the Renaissance improve?

Diagnosis and treatment had not advanced much since the Middle Ages. Just as before, physicians did not know or understand what caused diseases or how to cure them.

 ## In what ways were Renaissance treatments similar to previous periods?

Despite some advances, there will still 4 main aspects of continuity witnessed in Renaissance *(p.36)* medicine.

☑ People were still superstitious. It was believed that the touch of a king could cure people of diseases like scrofula.

☑ Doctors still hadn't understood the link between dirt and disease.

☑ There was continuity in ideas about what caused disease: for example, miasma.

☑ Herbal remedies remained popular.

☑ Bloodletting was still used as a treatment.

 ## How did treatment change during the Renaissance?

There were 4 key changes that happened to medicine during the Renaissance *(p.36)* period.

☑ Galen *(p.19)* no longer dominated scientific thought, as doctors began to challenge his ideas.

☑ Technology was gradually advancing so that new inventions, like the microscope, helped make more discoveries.

☑ Alchemy became popular, as people began to look at using chemicals for cures, rather than balancing the humours.

☑ The Theory of Transference became popular. This suggested that a disease could be transferred through contact with a plant or animal. People might rub a vegetable on their ailments, in the hope that the vegetable would catch it and take it away.

QUACKERY

The rise of fake medicine.

What was quack medicine?

Quack medicines made wild claims about their ability to prevent or cure illness and disease although they did not work. At best they were harmless, at worst they could be deadly.

When did quack medicine become popular?

Quack medicine became popular in Britain during the 17th and 18th centuries and was still being used into the 19th century.

Who sold quack medicine?

Quack medicine was sold by 'quacks'. These were travelling salesmen who would sell their wares and move on before the patient realised the medicine didn't work.

What ingredients were in quack medicine use?

Quack medicines were made using everyday ingredients. Brandy and opium were common ingredients but the medicines could contain rhubarb, herbs and spices, and even arsenic or lead.

What is an example of quack medicine?

A famous example of quack medicine was Daffy's Elixir. It claimed to cure gout, rheumatism, kidney stones and colic amongst a range of other things.

RENAISSANCE HOSPITALS - CHANGE & CONTINUITY

Renaissance hospitals were different to medieval hospitals

? What were hospitals like in the Renaissance?

Some hospitals during the Renaissance *(p.36)* were still controlled by the Church, but fewer than before. They were very different from the hospitals that existed previously.

How did hospitals change during the Renaissance?

During the Renaissance *(p.36)*, hospitals changed in 6 key ways.

- ☑ Hospitals were no longer just places where pilgrims, travellers and the elderly could rest and pray. Patients were given treatment, and records were kept to show how many people recovered.
- ☑ Physicians started to visit patients in the hospitals, where they carried out observations and recommended treatments.
- ☑ Hospitals began to have their own apothecaries and pharmacies to make medicines.
- ☑ Hospitals began to provide good food for patients to eat. Although it was no longer believed that diet affected the four humours, it was accepted that it was important to recover and maintain good health.
- ☑ People began to visit hospitals when they sustained injuries in order to have them treated.
- ☑ As King Henry VIII closed down monasteries during the Reformation, many hospitals also closed as they were run by the Church. It took some time for numbers to increase again, and many hospitals were subsequently run by charities.

DID YOU KNOW?

One of the most famous hospitals of the Renaissance is still around today.

The Hospital of Santa Maria Nuova in Florence, Italy, is still active today.

18TH CENTURY HOSPITALS - CHANGE AND CONTINUITY

More endowments mean better health care

How many hospitals were there in the 18th century?

During the English Reformation many hospitals were closed. There were just five hospitals in England by 1700.

Who funded 18th century hospitals?

In the 1700s a number of new hospitals were built which were often funded by wealthy businessmen. Guy's Hospital in London was funded in 1724 by Thomas Guy, an investor in the South Sea Company. The hospital is still open today.

How were 18th century hospitals an improvement over previous centuries?

There were 4 main changes to hospitals during this period.

- ☑ The sick were properly cared for, unlike during medieval times, when hospitals were just a place for them to rest.
- ☑ Doctors received proper training, as medical schools were often attached to hospitals.
- ☑ Individual wards were developed to care for those with different types of diseases and illnesses.
- ☑ Hospitals now included an apothecary *(p.23)* and a surgeon.

What specialist hospitals were developed in the 18th century?

The 18th century saw not only the development of general hospitals for the sick, but also specialist hospitals.

- ☑ In 1746, London's Lock Hospital for venereal (sexually transmitted) diseases was opened.
- ☑ In 1747, wards in Middlesex Hospital were designated specifically for pregnant women.
- ☑ In 1751, St Luke's Hospital became the second largest public hospital for the mentally ill.

What impact did the changes to hospitals in the 18th century have?

These changes to hospitals had 3 main impacts.

- ☑ By 1800, over 20,000 patients per year were treated at hospitals in London.
- ☑ People's thinking about illness and poverty shifted, and caring for those who were sick became more of a priority.
- ☑ The thinking developed that an evidence-based, scientific approach could conquer illness.

> **DID YOU KNOW?**
>
> In 2020, Guy's Hospital employed 17,100 members of staff.

PEST HOUSES

A way to quarantine those who were infected

What were pest houses?

Pest houses were set up for people suffering from extremely infectious diseases, like the plague.

THOMAS SYDENHAM

Identifying disease as a group of symptoms, rather than an imbalance in the individual

Who was Thomas Sydenham?

Thomas Sydenham was an English physician who advanced the use scientific processes in medicine.

What was Thomas Sydenham also known as?

Sydenham was known as 'the English Hippocrates *(p. 17)*'.

What was Thomas Sydenham's main idea?

Sydenham would not rely on medical books alone. He believed in observing the patients and recording their symptoms. This process allowed him to see patterns between illnesses and treatments.

What was the main contribution of Thomas Sydenham?

Sydenham classified diseases into different types, based on which symptoms each patient exhibited. He was able to show, for example, that measles and scarlet fever were different types of disease.

What was the name of Thomas Sydenham's book?

In 1676, Sydenham published 'Medical Observations'. It explained how illnesses and diseases had external causes, and were not the result of something internal such as unbalanced humours.

What was the significance of Thomas Sydenham?

Sydenham was important because he paved the way for future doctors to take a more scientific approach to medicine.

DID YOU KNOW?

Sydenham has been called the 'English Hippocrates'.

This was because he emphasised careful observations of the patient and detailed record-keeping.

ROYAL SOCIETY

A hub of medical ideas and new thinking

What is the Royal Society?

The Royal Society was an English institution the purpose of which was to promote and support scientific research. Its members were a group of influential scientists, and it was created with the approval of King Charles II.

When was the Royal Society created?

The Royal Society was created in November 1660, and still exists today.

What was the purpose of the Royal Society?

The purpose of the Royal Society was to promote scientific understanding by sharing knowledge.

How did the Royal Society spread its ideas?

The Royal Society published a journal called 'Philosophical Transactions'. It contained experiments and research from scientists. The work was written in English rather than Latin, so that more people could understand it. The journal is still in publication today.

What was the motto of the Royal Society?

The motto of the Royal Society was 'Nullius in verba', which means 'Take nobody's word for it'.

Was the Royal Society credible?

People took notice of the Royal Society because King Charles II gave it a Royal Charter in 1662. Having the king's support gave it credibility.

DID YOU KNOW?

Robert Hooke, who invented the microscope, was the original Curator of Experiments for the Royal Society.

COLLEGE OF PHYSICIANS

Oldest medical college in England

What was the College of Physicians?

The College of Physicians is the oldest medical college in England. During the Renaissance *(p.36)* most British doctors were trained there. They learned about Galen's *(p.19)* works and that disease was spread through miasmas.

When was the College of Physicians created?

The College of Physicians was set up in 1518.

How did the College of Physicians help medical progress?

Doctors received proper training and were given a licence if they were trained at the College of Physicians.

DID YOU KNOW?

The College of Physicians was a men-only affair!
Women were not allowed to join for the first four centuries it existed!

COMPANY OF BARBER-SURGEONS

Barber surgeons were seen as more professional.

What was the Company of Barber-Surgeons?

The Company of Barber-Surgeons regulated the profession.

What was the role of the Company of Barber-Surgeons?

The charter made the profession respectable and granted barber-surgeons four criminal corpses every year for dissection.

DID YOU KNOW?

It was officially established in 1504
The Company of Barber-Surgeons merged with the Fellowship of Surgeons to form the Company of Barbers and Surgeons.

JOHN HUNTER

The father of modern surgery.

Who was John Hunter?

John Hunter was a famous surgeon in the 18th century.

What were Hunter's contributions to medical progress?

Hunter made many contributions to medical progress through 4 key methods:

- ☑ Writing books.
- ☑ Teaching.
- ☑ The scientific method.
- ☑ Anatomical specimens.

How did Hunter's books contribute to medical progress?

Hunter's books contributed to medical progress in five ways:

- ☑ His books showed the theoretical knowledge needed to understand anatomy.
- ☑ His writings were based on observations and willingness to experiment.
- ☑ In 1771, he published 'The Natural History of Teeth'.
- ☑ His books were very popular. They were translated into several different languages.
- ☑ His book 'Blood Inflammation and Gunshot Wounds' put to rest the idea that gunshot wounds were poisoned.

How did Hunter's teaching contribute to medical progress?

After being admitted to the Company of Surgeons, Hunter established a large medical practice. Many other surgeons were trained to use the scientific methods he had developed. For example, Edward Jenner *(p.43)* trained with him.

How did Hunter's use of the scientific method contribute to medical progress?

Hunter's use of the scientific method helped contribute to medical progress in 5 key ways:

- ☑ He experimented on himself to prove that gonorrhoea and syphilis were different diseases by injecting himself with the diseases.
- ☑ He advocated detailed and thorough observation to those he taught.
- ☑ Hunter experimented on patients. Dissections of knees had taught him about aneurysms. He theorised that if he encouraged new blood vessels to develop by restricting the existing ones he would not need to amputate the leg.
- ☑ He tested his theory of aneurysms on animals and then on a patient, who was able to walk out of hospital six weeks later.

How did Hunter's use of specimens contribute to medical progress?

Hunter collected anatomical specimens to experiment on. For example, to study blood flow he used wax to inflate narrow blood vessels.

DID YOU KNOW?

You can see John Hunter's discoveries for yourself!
The Hunterian Museum is located in the Royal College of Surgeons in London.

Quizzes, amazing exam preparation tools and more at GCSEHistory.com

GREAT PLAGUE

A major epidemic in London

What was the Great Plague?

The Great Plague was the last major epidemic of bubonic plague in England.

When was the Great Plague?

The Great Plague lasted from 1665 to 1666.

How many people died during the Great Plague?

The Great Plague killed 100,000 people, almost a quarter of London's population.

What did people believe were the causes of the Great Plague?

Due to a lack of medical understanding at the time, there were 3 main theories about the causes of the Great Plague.

- ☑ People believed that God had sent the disease as punishment.
- ☑ People believed that miasmas or bad smells caused the disease.
- ☑ Many believed that an unusual alignment of planets caused the disease.

What were the remedies used against the Great Plague?

Measures and cures for the plague were often unusual and extreme and included 5 main measures.

- ☑ Physicians tried to balance their patients' humours, for example by bloodletting.
- ☑ Fires were lit in the streets to purify the air.
- ☑ Infected houses were quarantined. A red cross, and the words 'God have mercy upon us', were painted on the door.
- ☑ Public prayer and confession.
- ☑ Transference was also carried out: for example, by attaching a live chicken to the buboes.

How were quack doctors involved in the plague?

Quack doctors were people who had no medical training, but who charged people for treatment as if they were a physician or apothecary. *(p.23)*

What were the quack cures during the Great Plague?

Due to a lack of medical understanding, there were a number of quack cures for the Great Plague. Quack doctors sold different pills or herbal remedies that supposedly cured people, or protected them from the disease.

How did the government intervene to try to stop the spread the Great Plague?

The government enforced 5 key measures to try and prevent the disease spreading.

- ☑ They banned public meetings, fairs, and large funerals.
- ☑ Streets and alleyways were regularly cleaned.
- ☑ Dogs and cats were killed, because people believed they were spreading the disease.
- ☑ Plague victims had to be quarantined for 40 days.
- ☑ Carts travelled through the city to collect dead bodies.

What event is believed to have helped end the great plague?

Some people believe the Great Fire of London killed much of the plague bacteria, by killing the rats who carried the flea, which transmitted the disease.

 What new methods had been made since the Black Death to limit the spread of the Great Plague?

There were 5 important improvements made since the Black Death *(p.32)*, that helped fight the Great Plague.

☑ People began to recognise the connection between dirt and disease.

☑ Trade was stopped, and mass gatherings were banned.

☑ The England-Scotland border was closed, helping to limit the spread of the disease.

☑ Quarantine was more effective, as people stayed in their houses to stop the disease spreading.

☑ Dead bodies were collected, and buried in 'plague pits' that were six feet deep.

DID YOU KNOW?

During the Great Plague, Charles II and his advisors escaped London to the countryside.

For the eight months that they were there, while 100,000 Londoners died, they had three meetings about the Plague. Two were about how they could keep the king safe.

GREAT PLAGUE COMPARISON WITH BLACK DEATH

A comparison of the Black Death and the Great Plague

 Were there similarities and differences between the Black Death and the Great Plague?

Despite being separated by over 300 years, there were many similarities between the Black Death *(p.32)* of 1348 and the Great Plague *(p.51)* in 1665. This was because there had been very few medical developments that helped to explain the connection between germs and disease.

 What were the similarities between the Black Death and the Great Plague?

There were 3 main similarities between the Black Death *(p.32)* and the Great Plague *(p.51)*.

☑ Many still believed that God sent the disease as a punishment, or that it was caused by miasma.

☑ Many people moved to the countryside to avoid the larger, cramped cities.

☑ There was no cure for the disease, as doctors didn't understand the connection between germs and diseases.

 What were the differences between the Black Death and the Great Plague?

There were also 4 main differences between the Black Death *(p.32)* and the Great Plague *(p.51)*.

☑ Methods of preventing the spread of the plague in 1665 were more carefully planned, and the Mayor of London did more to help.

☑ During the Great Plague *(p.51)*, residents were ordered to sweep the streets in front of their houses, making the environment cleaner.

☑ When a person died, plague-searchers were sent to examine bodies and determine whether they had died from the plague. Their diagnosis was later confirmed by surgeons.

☑ In 1665, doctors and scientists had better understanding of the connection between dirt and disease, although they couldn't explain it.

THE ROLE OF THE INDIVIDUAL IN RENAISSANCE MEDICINE

The individual played an important role in the development of medicine

❓ What role did individuals play in medicine in the Renaissance?

There were a number of individuals who made very important discoveries in the period but they were often ignored by other physicians so this reduced their effect in developing medicine.

What are some examples of individuals influencing medicine in the Renaissance?

Here are 3 main examples of the role that the individual played:

☑ Paré treated war wounds and designed false limbs for soldiers.

☑ William Harvey *(p.41)* discovered that the heart pumped blood around the body.

☑ Da Vinci dissected over 30 bodies.

THE ROLE OF SCIENCE AND TECHNOLOGY IN RENAISSANCE MEDICINE

Science and Technology played an important role in the development of medicine

❓ What role did science and technology play in medicine in the Renaissance?

Science and technology was beginning to develop in this period so played a greater role in the development of health and medicine than in the medieval period.

What are some examples of science and technology influencing medicine in the Renaissance?

Here are 4 main examples of the role that the science and technology played:

☑ The printing press *(p.38)* was invented in around 1440.

☑ The microscope was invented in 1590.

☑ Surgeons' skills improved with opium used as an anaesthetic *(p.64)*, although an incorrect dose could kill a patient.

☑ The scientific method was becoming more popular.

THE ROLE OF THE GOVERNMENT IN RENAISSANCE MEDICINE

The government played an important role in the development of medicine

❓ What role did the government play in medicine in the Renaissance?

Government began to play a larger role in the development of medicine by introducing new laws so it became more important than in the medieval period.

What are some examples of the government influencing medicine in the Renaissance?

4 examples of the government influencing medicine in the Renaissance *(p.44)* are:

- ✅ The bodies of those who died from plague were brought out at night when fewer people were about.
- ✅ Henry VIII allowed the Company of Barber-Surgeons to be formed in 1540, controlling qualifications and ensuring standards were maintained.
- ✅ During the Great Plague *(p.51)* of 1665, homeowners were ordered to sweep the streets in front of their houses.
- ✅ During the Great Plague *(p.51)*, the government also banned large gatherings.

THE ROLE OF COMMUNICATION IN RENAISSANCE MEDICINE

Communication played an important role in the development of medicine

What role did communication play in medicine in the Renaissance?

Better communication meant ideas about medicine and surgery could be spread more easily in the Renaissance *(p.36)* so it was significant.

What are some examples of communication influencing medicine in the Renaissance?

Here are 3 main examples of the role that communication played:

- ✅ Medical knowledge spread more widely as traders explored new lands like America.
- ✅ The creation of the printing press *(p.38)* allowed for news books and ideas to be spread more quickly.
- ✅ In 1724, George Cheyne published his successful 'Essay on Health and Long Life'. This presented the argument that obesity was caused by a poor diet and lifestyle.

THE ROLE OF RELIGION IN RENAISSANCE MEDICINE

Religion played an important role in the development of medicine, however, during this period its role was diminishing

What role did religion play in medicine in the Renaissance?

Religion continued to play a very important role in medicine. For example, the ideas of Galen *(p.19)* were still supported by the Church. However, scientific ideas did begin to challenge the teachings of the Church.

What role did the factor of religion play in medicine in the Renaissance?

Here are 4 main examples of the role that religion played:

- ✅ People were no longer reliant on monks to copy out books by hand.
- ✅ Many still believed the Plague was God's punishment.
- ✅ Surgeons had more freedom to carry out human dissections to learn more about anatomy.
- ✅ Henry VIII seized the wealth of Catholic monasteries and gave money to start hospitals.

THE ROLE OF WAR IN RENAISSANCE MEDICINE

War played an important role in the development of medicine and was one of the most important factors during the Renaissance

? **What role did war play in medicine in the Renaissance?**

War played an important role in the development of medicine and surgery during the Renaissance *(p.36)*. The development of gunpowder meant there was a wide range of new wounds to treat.

What are some examples of war influencing medicine in the Renaissance?

There are 2 main examples of the role that war played in medicine during the Renaissance *(p.36)*.

- ☑ Ambroise Paré ran out of oil during a 1537 battle and improvised a soothing cream. This healed wounds quickly and was less painful.
- ☑ Paré came up with a new method of amputation, tying strings around blood vessels instead of cauterising.

THE ROLE OF CHANCE IN RENAISSANCE MEDICINE

Chance played an important role in the development of medicine

? **What role did chance play in medicine in the Renaissance?**

Some new discoveries happened by chance when people were not necessarily looking for them, although overall it played a small role in the development of medicine during the Renaissance *(p.36)*.

What are some examples of chance influencing medicine in the Renaissance?

Here is 1 main example of the role that chance played:

- ☑ Ambroise Paré ran out of hot oil in 1537 which resulted in his improvisation of a cream of rose oil, egg white and turpentine to heal the wounds.

LAISSEZ-FAIRE

'Let it be'

? **What was laissez-faire?**

Laissez-faire, a French term that translates as 'let it be', was the idea that the government should take a hands-off approach to public health.

18TH AND 19TH CENTURY CAUSES - CHANGE AND CONTINUITY

New ideas gather pace

What was the understanding of disease in the 19th century?

In the mid-nineteenth century, understanding of disease was based on miasma and spontaneous generation.

What did people believe about miasma and disease in the 19th century?

People still believed that disease was carried through bad air.

What was the understanding of spontaneous generation in the 19th century?

Spontaneous generation was a theory that rotting material - such as food and excrement - created microorganisms, which caused miasma and disease.

Why did the understanding of disease not progress in the 19th century?

There were 2 main factors affecting medical progress and understanding in the mid-nineteenth century.

☑ Hospitals relied on charity for funding. There was generally little money available for research.

☑ Doctors wanted to continue to work as they always had, and were reluctant to try new methods for treating patients.

What were the main changes that led to understanding disease in the nineteenth century?

There were 5 main changes that allowed for medical progress in the 19th century.

☑ The development of microscopes allowed Louis Pasteur *(p.59)* to develop and publish his germ theory *(p.59)* in 1861.

☑ Supernatural *(p.16)* and religious ideas about disease were dying out.

☑ More hospitals were built, and the work of Florence Nightingale *(p.57)* meant they were a lot cleaner.

☑ The development of anaesthetics and antiseptics led to improvements in surgery.

☑ The government began to take more action and implemented measures to improve public health.

DID YOU KNOW?

There were 'cholera riots' during the first cholera outbreak in 1831.

People were angry at having their movement limited, and being unable to visit their loved ones in cholera hospitals.

19TH CENTURY HOSPITALS

Slow progress was made

What were hospitals like in the 19th century?

In the early 1800s, hospitals were small organisations that relied on private or charitable funding. However, the pressure to provide medical care resulted in the establishment of general hospitals.

What alternatives to hospitals were available in the nineteenth century?

Hospitals were difficult to get into so alternatives included:

- ☑ A home visit from a doctor who would diagnose the illness and suggest a treatment.
- ☑ The patient's family, or a nurse if they could afford one, would take care of the patient at home. They were expected to ensure that the patient received the treatment, and to keep records of their condition.

How were patients treated in 19th century hospitals?

Hospital patients had to follow rules and behave in a certain way during their stay. Sometimes they were only admitted with a recommendation, written by a doctor or a respected member of the community.

What types of hospitals were there in the 19th century?

There were 3 main types of hospitals in the 19th century.

- ☑ Cottage hospitals, accommodating about 12 patients, were set up from the mid-19th century. They would be run by a local GP.
- ☑ Infirmaries were larger hospitals built in towns and cities. These also provided an outpatient service. Initially they were funded by charities, and were often crowded and dirty.
- ☑ As well as general infirmaries, specialist hospitals were also built, such as the Hospital for Sick Children in Great Ormond Street, which was established in 1852.

DID YOU KNOW?

Starting to resemble what we know today!

Hospitals were beginning to change from places that gave basic care to the sick, to places that were trying to treat disease and carry out basic surgery.

FLORENCE NIGHTINGALE

The Lady with the Lamp

Who was Florence Nightingale?

Born in 1820, Florence Nightingale became a nurse despite opposition from her family. She cared for patients during the Crimean War, and is often to referred to as the 'Lady with the Lamp'.

What was nursing and hospital care like before Florence Nightingale?

In the early 1800s, most people were cared for by family in their own homes. A doctor would visit the patient and prescribe them medicine. Nurses were untrained and did not keep records on patient care.

Why did Nightingale's family not want her to become a nurse?

Prior to Florence Nightingale's influence in the mid-nineteenth century, nursing had a bad reputation, and nurses required no skills or training.

What did Florence Nightingale do in the Crimean War?

In 1854, during the Crimean War, she went to the Scutari Hospital Barracks in Turkey with a team of 38 nurses, to care for wounded soldiers.

What problems did Florence Nightingale face upon arrival in the Crimea?

Conditions were terrible for the 10,000 patients, and disease and infection were widespread. Medical supplies were limited, wards were filthy and infested with pests, and the food was poor.

What were Florence Nightingale's contributions to medicine?

She implemented measures that significantly improved hygiene at Scutari. This included cleaning surfaces, washing bedding, and ensuring the kitchens were clean. The quality of the food given to patients was improved, and windows were opened to allow air to circulate.

Why did Florence Nightingale make changes at Scutari?

Nightingale believed that miasmas were the cause of illness and that they would be prevented by keeping places clean.

What impact did Florence Nightingale's actions have at Scutari?

It's believed her actions resulted in the death rate falling from 42% to just 2%. She also became very popular both in the hospital and back in Britain.

What happened when Florence Nightingale returned from war?

Press coverage of her work in Scutari made Florence Nightingale famous. When she returned to Britain in 1856 she was considered an expert on nursing and hospitals.

What were Florence Nightingale's achievements?

Florence Nightingale's achievements after she returned from Scutari included writing over 200 books and creating training schools for nurses.

- ☑ In 1859, she wrote the book 'Notes on Nursing', which became a bestseller.
- ☑ The Nightingale Fund was created, which raised over £44,000. She used the money to set up a training school at St Thomas's Hospital in 1860, and a training school for midwives at King's College Hospital in 1861.
- ☑ She played an important role in promoting the French pavilion-design of hospitals, with wider open spaces to prevent miasma, which made them cleaner and safer.

What impact did Florence Nightingale have on hospitals?

In 'Notes from Nursing', Florence Nightingale set out her ideas about how hospitals were organised.

- ☑ She recommended building hospitals using a design developed in France. The design was based around the pavilion system, to ensure good ventilation through the wards which separated patients, in order to prevent the spread of contagious diseases.
- ☑ She suggested large windows to let in light and air.
- ☑ She also suggested surfaces should be easier to clean, such as tiled floors and painted walls.
- ☑ In 1868, St Thomas' Hospital (where the Nightingale School of Nurses was located) was rebuilt according to Nightingale's recommendations.

What changes did Florence Nightingale bring to nursing?

There were 4 important changes that Florence Nightingale brought to nursing.

- ☑ In 1860, Florence Nightingale opened the Nightingale School For Nurses at St Thomas' Hospital.
- ☑ This introduced strict rules for nurses - they had to go to bed at a certain time, and write a report on their progress every week.
- ☑ It gave nurses a formal training.
- ☑ It raised the status of nursing to a popular profession. By 1900, there were 68,000 trained nurses in Britain.

Why is Nightingale significant?

Florence Nightingale is regarded the founder of modern nursing. She turned nursing into a respectable profession, and introduced patient care and cleanliness to hospitals.

DID YOU KNOW?

Florence Nightingale did not support the idea of female doctors.

Writing about them in 1860, she said that they 'have only tried to be men and have only succeeded in becoming third-rate men'.

LOUIS PASTEUR'S GERM THEORY

'Chance only favours prepared minds.'
Louis Pasteur

Who was Louis Pasteur?

Louis Pasteur was a French scientist who discovered germs and proved a direct connection between germs and disease.

When was Pasteur's germ theory published?

Louis Pasteur published his work on germ theory in 1861. In 1878, he published the next stage of his theory - that germs caused infection.

What was Pasteur's germ theory?

This was the theory that germs caused disease. It disproved previous beliefs about other causes, such as miasma.

What are the principles Pasteur's theory?

There were four basic principles of germ theory.

- ✅ The air contains living microorganisms.
- ✅ Microbes in the air cause decay.
- ✅ Microbes are not evenly distributed in the air.
- ✅ Microbes can be killed by heating them.

What led to Pasteur's germ theory?

In 1857, Pasteur was employed by a French brewery to work out why their beer kept going sour.

How did Pasteur make his discovery?

Using a microscope, he discovered microorganisms growing in the liquid. He realised that sterilising water, and keeping it in a sealed flask, prevented microorganisms from entering it. If the sterilised water was kept in an open flask, the microbes would breed again.

What was Pasteur's process of 'pasteurisation'?

Pasteur called the process of heating liquid to kill bacteria 'pasteurisation'.

How did Pasteur make the link between germs and disease?

In 1865, Pasteur was asked to investigate a problem in the silk industry. He discovered that silkworms were dying from microorganisms and subsequently made the link between germs and disease.

Why did doctors oppose Pasteur's theory?

Because microorganisms could be seen everywhere, for example in human blood, doctors could not understand why some caused disease and others did not.

What was the impact of Pasteur's germ theory?

There were 4 main results of germ theory.

- ☑ It demonstrated the belief that disease was created by spontaneous generation was wrong. However, spontaneous generation was still an influential idea that some doctors, such as Dr Henry Bastian, still supported.
- ☑ Between 1876 and 1883, Robert Koch (p.61) discovered that different bacteria cause different diseases.
- ☑ It led to an understanding of why infection occurred in surgery.
- ☑ It led to Lister's use of carbolic acid (p.67) as an antiseptic (p.67) in surgery.

How did Pasteur discover a vaccine for chicken cholera?

The chicken cholera (p.71) vaccine was discovered by chance in 1879. A mistake by Pasteur's assistant led to the realisation that the germ was weakened when exposed to air. Injecting the weakened germ into chickens stopped them from catching the disease.

How did Pasteur help the development of vaccines?

Pasteur helped discover two other vaccines.

- ☑ In 1881, Pasteur's team produced a weakened strain of anthrax that would prevent the disease in sheep.
- ☑ In 1885, Pasteur successfully cured a boy from rabies by using a vaccine for the disease he had developed.

How did Pasteur's rivalry with Koch lead to scientific breakthroughs?

There are 5 main reasons why the rivalry between Pasteur and Koch (p.61) led to scientific breakthroughs.

- ☑ Both were researching during the Franco-Prussian War, and defeating diseases could have a big impact on the battlefield.
- ☑ The governments of France and Germany paid for the laboratories and teams of scientists, for Pasteur and Koch (p.61) respectively.
- ☑ The individual characters of both men played a role. Both were relentless in their attempts to make scientific advances. For Pasteur, this resulted in his scientific breakthrough about germ theory; and for Koch (p.61) it resulted in his discoveries about tuberculosis (TB) and cholera (p.71).
- ☑ Communication increased the rivalry, as Koch (p.61) heard about Pasteur's discoveries quickly, helping him to make breakthroughs of his own.
- ☑ Teamwork and rivalry contributed to breakthroughs, as both sides quickly wanted to discover vaccinations for contagious diseases such as diphtheria.

DID YOU KNOW?

Three of Louis Pasteur's five children died of typhoid.

Quizzes, amazing exam preparation tools and more at GCSEHistory.com

JOHN TYNDALL

A defender of Pasteur.

Who was Tyndall?

John Tyndall was an Irish physicist in the 19th century.

What did John Tyndall do?

John Tyndall helped germ theory *(p.59)* become accepted.

How did John Tyndall help germ theory become accepted?

Tyndall helped germ theory *(p.59)* become accepted in 2 main ways:

- ☑ He lectured on dust and disease by experimenting with light to show tiny microbes in the air.
- ☑ In 1876, he delivered a speech to British doctors on Koch's *(p.61)* discoveries about anthrax.

DID YOU KNOW?

Tyndall was born into a poor family.

He was born into a poor Protestant family in Ireland, but despite this he was able to make a remarkable contribution to medicine.

ROBERT KOCH

Taking germ theory to the next level

Who was Robert Koch?

Robert Koch was a German doctor considered to be the founder of modern bacteriology.

What were Koch's achievements?

Koch's work was important for 3 main reasons.

- ☑ He developed a method for staining and photographing microorganisms using dye.
- ☑ He discovered the specific germs that caused a number of diseases: anthrax in 1876, tuberculosis in 1882, and cholera *(p.71)* in 1883.
- ☑ He developed the use of agar jelly for growing bacterial cultures on which he could experiment.
- ☑ He developed a steam steriliser which used heat to sterilise equipment and dressings.

How did Koch prove that cholera was spread through contaminated water?

In 1884, he found cholera *(p.71)* in drinking water in Calcutta, India, which proved it was spread in water supplies. This confirmed John Snow's *(p.72)* theory of why cholera had spread in London in 1854.

What was the significance of Koch's work?

Koch's work was a major breakthrough and he had 2 key impacts on medicine.

- ☑ Doctors began to study disease itself, rather than studying and treating symptoms.

✅ He made it easier for other scientists to identify and study bacteria, such as diphtheria and pneumonia, because of his staining technique.

Why were Koch and Pasteur rivals?

Koch and Pasteur *(p.59)* were rivals for two key reasons:

✅ They fell out at an 1882 conference over a mistranslated term in Pasteur's *(p.59)* lecture. Two of Koch's students then wrote a long paper criticising Pasteur's findings on anthrax.

✅ Their countries were at war between 1870-71, and their respective governments gave them funding for research and equipment.

DID YOU KNOW?

Pasteur and Koch were rivals, and didn't get on.

They fell out at an 1882 conference over a mistranslated term in Pasteur's lecture. Two of Koch's students then wrote a long paper criticising Pasteur's findings on anthrax.

WILLIAM ROBERTS

Developed the germ theory.

Who was William Roberts?

William Roberts was a Welsh physician.

What was Roberts' contribution to medicine?

Roberts criticised spontaneous generation and developed a doctor's version of germ theory *(p.59)*.

What did Roberts do to enhance germ theory?

Roberts helped advance germ theory *(p.59)* in 2 ways:

✅ He created a link between laboratory research performed by scientists, and the practical evidence of surgeons and public health doctors.

✅ He publicised Koch's *(p.61)* work on germs and their role in infections.

DID YOU KNOW?

Surgery was a family business. Robert's father was a surgeon.

WILLIAM CHEYNE
Supporter of the germ theory

Who was William Cheyne?
William Cheyne was a Scottish surgeon and bacteriologist.

What was Cheyne's contribution to medicine?
Cheyne supported germ theory *(p.59)* and helped it become accepted.

How did Cheyne help germ theory become accepted?
Cheyne helped germ theory *(p.59)* become accepted by:

- ☑ Translating Koch's *(p.61)* work into English.
- ☑ Publishing a paper discussing Koch's *(p.61)* findings.
- ☑ Arguing that some microbes in healthy tissue and wounds are harmless and do not always lead to disease.

> **DID YOU KNOW?**
>
> Cheyne went to art school but dropped out to become a doctor!

SURGERY IN THE 19TH CENTURY
Bloody and brutal!

What was surgery like in the nineteenth century?
Surgery in the mid-19th century was basic, dangerous, and had a low survival rate.

Why did so many people die in surgery before the late nineteenth century?
Surgery in the mid-19th century had a high mortality rate for 3 main reasons.

- ☑ It was painful, which caused some patients to go into shock and die. It was also hard for them to keep still, and surgeons had to work very fast, which increased the likelihood of mistakes.
- ☑ The wounds created by surgery were likely to become infected.
- ☑ Many patients bled to death.

What pain relief was used for surgery at the beginning of the nineteenth century?
Surgeons used various methods to try and prevent pain in the mid-nineteenth century. These included knocking patients out, giving them alcohol to make them drunk, or giving them opium. None were effective.

What was surgery like in the early nineteenth century?
Patients would usually be held down, and the operation performed as quickly as possible to reduce the amount of pain experienced. Operations often took place in the patient's home.

Why did surgery improve in the late nineteenth century?

The 19th century experienced 4 key changes for surgery.

- ☑ In 1861, Louis Pasteur *(p.59)* discovered that diseases were caused by germs, paving the way for antiseptic *(p.67)*, and later aseptic, surgery *(p.68)*.
- ☑ Joseph Lister's carbolic acid *(p.67)* spray in 1865 killed germs before and during surgery, reducing infection with antiseptic *(p.67)* surgery.
- ☑ James Blundell carried out early blood transfusions, publishing his paper 'Experiments on the Transfusion of Blood by the Syringe' in 1818.
- ☑ In 1847, James Simpson's discovery of chloroform *(p.66)* reduced pain in surgery, particularly for childbirth.

DID YOU KNOW?

They liked to see pus!

Pus was not seen as a warning sign, rather it was seen as a good thing, and evidence that a wound was healing!

ANAESTHETICS

A new way to help relieve pain.

 What were anaesthetics?

Anaesthetics were developed during the 1800s to make surgery less painful for the patient.

 What types of anaesthetics were used in the nineteenth century?

The use of 3 significant anaesthetics were developed in the nineteenth century:

- ☑ Nitrous oxide *(p.65)*.
- ☑ Ether *(p.65)*.
- ☑ Chloroform *(p.66)*.

DID YOU KNOW?

Anaesthetic was also used in dentistry

Ether was first used by William T G Morton to remove a tumour from a young man's neck.

HOW PAIN WAS CONQUERED - NITROUS OXIDE

The funniest anaesthetic.

? What was nitrous oxide?

Nitrous oxide, also known as laughing gas, is an anaesthetic *(p.64)*. It was considered too weak to be suitable for major surgical operations.

Who discovered nitrous oxide?

Humphry Davy discovered the anaesthetic *(p.64)* properties of nitrous oxide, although it was American dentist Horace Wells who first used it as an anaesthetic to extract a tooth.

When was nitrous oxide first used as an anaesthetic?

Nitrous oxide was first used as an anaesthetic *(p.64)* in 1844.

DID YOU KNOW?

Nitrous Oxide is a colourless gas.

HOW PAIN WAS CONQUERED - ETHER

A dangerous anaesthetic.

? What was ether?

Ether was an anaesthetic. *(p.64)*

Why wasn't ether more widely used?

Ether was an effective form of pain relief, but had unpleasant side effects (such as vomiting). It was also highly flammable.

When was ether first successfully used in surgery?

Ether was first used successfully in 1846, in a leg amputation.

Who first used ether successfully?

Robert Liston *(p.66)* first used ether successfully in Britain.

DID YOU KNOW?

Despite its extreme flammability, ether is still used as an anaesthetic in some developing countries.

ROBERT LISTON

'The fastest knife in the West End.'

Who was Robert Liston?

Robert Liston was a surgeon renowned for his speed and strength. He once amputated a leg in 28 seconds. Liston was the first to use ether *(p.65)* as an anaesthetic *(p.64)* during surgery.

HOW PAIN WAS CONQUERED - CHLOROFORM

A controversial painkiller.

What is chloroform?

Chloroform was an effective form of pain relief.

Who was the first doctor to use chloroform during surgery?

James Simpson, a professor of midwifery at Edinburgh University, experimented with chloroform on himself and friends.

When did James Simpson discover that chloroform could be used as an anaesthetic?

James Simpson discovered that chloroform could be used as an anaesthetic *(p.64)* in 1847.

How did James Simpson first use chloroform?

James Simpson used chloroform on women in childbirth.

Why was there opposition to the use of chloroform?

There were 3 main reasons why some people opposed the use of chloroform.

- ☑ Some army surgeons believed that soldiers should endure pain.
- ☑ Some religious people believed it was God's intention that women should feel pain in childbirth, and that suffering during surgery was God's will.
- ☑ It was difficult to get the dosage right. This was demonstrated when 14-year-old Hannah Greener died while having an ingrown toenail removed.

Who made chloroform more popular?

Chloroform finally became accepted when Queen Victoria used it during the delivery of her eighth child. After this, patients began to ask for it in their operations.

Why was the use of chloroform dangerous?

Chloroform led to the so-called Black Period of surgery, when death rates increased because, with unconscious patients, surgeons were taking their time and doing more advanced surgeries. This meant they were unknowingly taking infection deeper into the body.

How was chloroform use made safer?

John Snow *(p.72)* developed a type of chloroform inhaler and calculated the correct dose per patient, making it much safer and preventing an overdose.

ANTISEPTICS

Substances to kill the germs

What are antiseptics?

Antiseptics are subtances used to kill microorganisms and prevent infection.

When were antiseptics developed?

Understanding of infection increased during the 1840s with the work of Ignaz Semmelweis. The first antiseptic, carbolic acid *(p.67)*, was used by Joseph Lister in 1865.

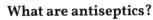

CARBOLIC ACID

An effective antiseptic

What was carbolic acid?

Carbolic acid, or phenol, wasthe first true antiseptic *(p.67)* used in surgery.

How was carbolic acid discovered?

Joseph Lister studied Pasteur's *(p.59)* germ theory *(p.59)* and, after realising carbolic acid was effective in stopping wounds from turning gangrenous, he developed a carbolic acid spray to kill germs on both medical instruments and the wound.

When was carbolic acid first used?

Joseph Lister first used carbolic acid, in the form of a spray, in 1865.

How was carbolic acid used in antiseptic surgery.

Antiseptic *(p.67)* surgery involved cleaning surgical instruments, and the patient's wounds, with carbolic acid.

What results did Lister achieve by using carbolic acid?

By using Lister's antiseptic *(p.67)* techniques, the death rate among patients who had amputations dropped from 46% to 15%.

Why was Lister criticised for his use of carbolic acid?

There were 5 main reasons why there was opposition to Lister's methods.

☑ Carbolic acid made the instruments tricky to hold, because they were slippery.

- ☑ Carbolic acid was unpleasant to use, as it irritated surgeons' hands.
- ☑ Doctors applied Lister's methods incorrectly, leading them to believe his theory was wrong.
- ☑ The equipment was expensive to buy and set up.
- ☑ Lister was arrogant, and disliked by many of the surgical community.

 Why did Lister use catgut soaked in carbolic acid?

Lister used catgut as a ligature. It could be soaked in carbolic acid, which helped prevent infection in the wound.

DID YOU KNOW?

Joseph Lister came across the idea of carbolic acid because it was used on fields to neutralise the smell of the sewage used as fertiliser.

He realised that it would be safe to use because it didn't hurt the animals that then grazed on the land.

ASEPTIC SURGERY

Surgery performed under sterilised conditions

 What is aseptic surgery?

Aseptic surgery ensures that operations are carried out in sterile conditions.

 What was the difference between antiseptic and aseptic surgery?

Antiseptic *(p.67)* surgery destroys germs on a surgeon's hands, instruments, and immediate surroundings using chemicals e.g. carbolic acid *(p.67)*. Aseptic surgery aims to achieve a completely sterile environment, free from germs, using a combination of measures such as heat and antiseptics.

 When was aseptic surgery established?

Aseptic surgery had become common by the year 1900.

 What methods were used in aseptic surgery?

There were four key elements to aseptic surgery.

- ☑ Surgeons were scrubbed clean before operating. Today, modern surgeons still 'scrub in' before going into theatre.
- ☑ Surgeons wore new clothes and a fresh pair of thin rubber gloves for each operation.
- ☑ All instruments used during surgery were sterilised beforehand, using steam.
- ☑ The size of operating theatres got smaller, to reduce the risk of infection, and spectators were no longer allowed.

INDUSTRIALISATION

Lice, poor ventilation and dirty water cause ill-health

What was public health like in the mid-nineteenth century?

Industrialisation had a huge negative impact on public health and living conditions. It led to overcrowding and increased the spread of disease.

How did housing conditions affect public health in industrial Britain?

Houses were built cheaply and as close together as possible. They were usually damp, with little light or ventilation.

How did sanitary conditions affect public health in industrial Britain?

There was usually an inadequate supply of clean water, and poor removal of sewage and rubbish. One toilet could be used by 100 people.

DID YOU KNOW?

The food available in nineteenth century towns was often impure.

It was common for milk to be watered down with added chalk and for butter to be coloured with copper.

EDWIN CHADWICK

A civil servant reports on public health

Who was Edwin Chadwick?

Edwin Chadwick was a civil servant who was involved with the workhouses. He was asked by the government to report on the living conditions and health of the poor.

What was Chadwick's report called?

Chadwick's report, called 'Report on the Sanitary Conditions of the Labouring Population', was published in 1842.

What conclusions did Chadwick claim in his report?

Edwin Chadwick's report reached 4 main conclusions:

- ☑ Ill-health was caused by the awful conditions in which people lived.
- ☑ If towns were cleaner, there wouldn't be as much disease, and people would not have to take time off work. This would result in fewer people needing the workhouses, which would save ratepayers money.
- ☑ Clean water and sewage disposal was needed for a healthy nation.

Why did Chadwick suggest people could save money by looking after the poor?

Local governments should be responsible for public health and set up boards of health. People would pay taxes to pay for this; but it would save money in the long term, as living conditions improved and fewer people used workhouses.

What did Chadwick recommend to improve health?

Chadwick made two recommendations to address poor living conditions as a cause of disease.

- ☑ A drainage system and refuse collections should be organised.
- ☑ A medical officer should be appointed to each area.

How did the government react to Chadwick's proposals?

Chadwick's ideas about increasing rates were not popular. It was not until there was a further cholera *(p.71)* epidemic that the government began to act on his recommendations.

> **DID YOU KNOW?**
>
> **Politicians and civil servants who agreed with the Chadwick's ideas, and wanted better public health, were known as the 'Clean Party'.**
>
> The group of politicians and civil servants who believed that health was not the government's responsibility were known as the 'Dirty Party'.

FIRST PUBLIC HEALTH ACT

Encouraging towns to improve public health

What was the Public Health Act of 1848?

The 1848 Public Health Act was the first attempt by the government to enforce the clean up of towns in England and Wales.

What did the Public Health Act 1848 recommend?

The 1848 Public Health Act made four main recommendations.

- ☑ Each town could appoint a Medical Officer of Health.
- ☑ A general Board of Health could be set up, and towns would be allowed to create their own local boards of health.
- ☑ Rubbish removals could be organised, and a sewer system built.
- ☑ People should have access to clean water.

What were the problems with the Public Health Act of 1848?

The Public Health Act had of 1848 had limited impact. There were two main reasons for this.

- ☑ The terms of the Act were only temporary.
- ☑ The Act was voluntary. To create a local board of health required 10% of ratepayers to be in favour, and some local authorities did not take action.

What was the significance of the Public Health Act 1848?

This was the first time the government had passed a law to improve public health, and demonstrates the move away from a laissez-faire *(p.55)* attitude.

KING CHOLERA
The 'Blue Death'

What is cholera?

Cholera is a potentially deadly disease that causes severe sickness, diarrhoea and dehydration.

What was cholera's nickname?

Cholera was nicknamed 'the blue death' as it ruptured blood vessels, and skin turned blue as people became dehydrated.

When were there outbreaks of cholera?

Cholera first arrived in Britain in 1831. There were further outbreaks in 1848 *(p.70)*, 1853, and 1865.

How many people died in each outbreak of cholera?

The number of deaths varied in each outbreak:

- ☑ In 1831-32, London suffered 5,275 deaths. In total, the outbreak killed 21,882 across Britain.
- ☑ In 1848 *(p.70)*-49, 53,292 people died.
- ☑ In 1853-54, 20,097 people died.
- ☑ In 1865-66, 14,378 people died.

Who discovered the causes for cholera?

A doctor called John Snow *(p.72)*.

How did John Snow discover the cause of cholera?

Snow *(p.72)* studied deaths from cholera and made a map of them. He traced the source of the outbreak to a water pump on Broad Street, London.

When was the cause of cholera discovered?

The cause of cholera was discovered in 1854.

What did John Snow think about the causes of cholera?

As many of the victims of the 1854 outbreak lived near a water pump on Broad Street, Snow *(p.72)* theorised that cholera could not be caused by miasma and was instead spread by contaminated water.

What was done to prevent the spread of cholera?

The government had a laissez-faire *(p.55)* attitude, which meant that they stayed out of public health issues. As a result, people tried 2 main ways to prevent cholera:

- ☑ Many thought it was caused by miasma, so tried to prevent it by cleaning up dirty streets.
- ☑ In 1848 *(p.70)*, the first Public Health Act suggested that towns and cities provide clean water supplies. However, as it was not compulsory, its impact was limited.

 ### Why was there opposition to John Snow's discovery of the cause of cholera?

Some doctors disagreed with Snow's *(p.72)* findings. Pasteur's *(p.59)* germ theory *(p.59)* had not been published so Snow's idea that cholera was transmitted through contaminated water, rather than through miasma could not be proven.

 ### How was the cholera outbreak of 1854 ended?

Snow *(p.72)* asked for the handle of the Broad Street water pump to be removed, so people could not use it. The outbreak quickly ended, proving the disease had come from the water in the pump. It was later found that a cesspit had been leaking into the well.

 ### Why were Snow's cholera findings important?

John Snow *(p.72)* had 2 main impacts.

- ☑ In 1855, he presented the results of his investigation to Parliament, and suggested that a new sewer system was built, something the government later agreed to.
- ☑ Snow *(p.72)* proved that cholera was not carried through the air like a poisonous gas or miasma.

DID YOU KNOW?

A cholera victim could expel up to 20 litres of diarrhoea.

JOHN SNOW

The Father of Modern Epidemiology

 ### Who was John Snow?

John Snow was the doctor responsible for discovering that cholera *(p.71)* was a water-borne disease.

 ### What else did John Snow discover?

John Snow also invented an inhaler that could be used to administer chloroform *(p.66)* safely by controlling the dose.

DID YOU KNOW?

John Snow was the doctor responsible for Queen Victoria using chloroform during the birth of her eighth child.

After this, Victoria referred to it as 'that blessed chloroform!'. This contributed to the public acceptance of the use of the anaesthetic.

Quizzes, amazing exam preparation tools and more at GCSEHistory.com

THE GREAT STINK

The filthy River Thames becomes impossible to ignore

What was the Great Stink?

A heatwave in the summer of 1858 caused the River Thames to smell much worse than it usually did, due to the evaporation of water. As a result, the river had a more concentrated sewage content.

How did Parliament react to the Great Stink?

The smell was so bad that politicians in the Houses of Parliament, next to the river, demanded to meet somewhere else. MPs asked for help from Joseph Bazalgette *(p.73)*, a civil engineer.

What was the significance of the Great Stink?

The Great Stink of 1858 had 2 main effects.

- ☑ The sewer system beneath London was built, which greatly improved conditions in the city.
- ☑ The Great Stink marked the end of the laissez-faire *(p.55)* attitude of government.

DID YOU KNOW?

Temperatures during the summer of 1858 reached over 30 degrees celsius.

JOSEPH BAZALGETTE

Master engineer builds the London sewers

Who was Joseph Bazalgette?

Joseph Bazalgette was a civil engineer in the 1800s.

What was Bazalgette's contribution to public health?

He was the chief designer and engineer on London's sewer system, ordered after the Great Stink *(p.73)*.

What was Bazalgette's sewer system like?

It was designed to remove waste from London's streets by carrying waste downriver towards the sea. The main sewers covered a distance of 83 miles and removed 420 million gallons of sewage per day.

When was Bazalgette's sewer system built?

The system was offically opened in 1865, although the systme continued to be developed into the 1870s.

How much did Bazalgette's sewer system cost?

The system cost £3 million.

SECOND PUBLIC HEALTH ACT

Forcing towns to improve public health

What was the Public Health Act of 1875?

The second Public Health Act of 1875 was the government's attempt to enforce action to reduce some public health-related illnesses and diseases, such as cholera *(p.71)*.

Why did the government pass the Public Health Act 1875?

The second Public Health Act of 1875 was passed as the government began to realise that public health was part of their responsibility.

What measures were in the 1875 Public Health Act?

The Public Health Act of 1875 made local authorities responsible for 3 main areas of public health measures.

- ✅ There must be provision of clean water and proper disposal of rubbish and sewage.
- ✅ Medical Officers of Health should be appointed in every area.
- ✅ There were standards for new housing, and lodging houses should be checked.

Why was the 1875 Public Health Act an improvement on the 1848 Public Health Act?

The 1875 Health Act was different from the 1848 *(p.70)* Health Act because it was compulsory - local authorities were forced to carry out the improvements.

Why was the 1875 Public Health Act significant?

The second act signified a change in the government's laissez-faire *(p.55)* attitude. Laws were now being passed to improve public health and they had to be obeyed.

THE ROLE OF THE INDIVIDUAL IN 18TH AND 19TH CENTURY

MEDICINE

The individual played an important role in the development of medicine and was probably one of the most important factors during this time.

What role did the individual play in medicine in the 18th and 19th centuries?

Individual genius led to a lot of discoveries and progress within medicine and surgery in the 18th and 19th centuries so it was a highly significant factor.

What are some examples of individuals influencing medicine in the 18th and 19th century?

Here are some examples of the role that the individual played:

- ☑ Edward Jenner *(p.43)* created a vaccine for smallpox.
- ☑ Reformers like Florence Nightingale *(p.57)* argued that cleaning up the medical environment would stop diseases.
- ☑ John Snow *(p.72)* discovered that cholera *(p.71)* was caused by drinking dirty water.

THE ROLE OF SCIENCE AND TECHNOLOGY IN 18TH AND 19TH CENTURY MEDICINE

Science and technology played an important role in the development of medicine.

What role did science and technology play in medicine in the 18th and 19th centuries?

Science and technology advanced greatly in this period so medicine and surgery progressed rapidly. It was very important.

What are some examples of science and technology influencing medicine in the 18th and 19th century?

Here are some examples of the role that science and technology played.

- ☑ Koch *(p.61)* developed a technique of identifying a germ in diseased animals, then identifying and dyeing it.
- ☑ Jenner's *(p.43)* vaccination was safer than inoculation.
- ☑ The first X-ray *(p.79)* machine was invented in 1895.

THE ROLE OF THE GOVERNMENT IN 18TH AND 19TH CENTURY MEDICINE

The government played an important role in the development of medicine and during this time their influence increased.

What role did the government play in medicine in the 18th and 19th centuries?

During the 19th century the government introduced a wide range of new laws to improve public health. It became extremely significant.

What are some examples of the government influencing medicine in the 18th and 19th century?

Here are some examples of the role that the government played.

☑ Koch *(p.61)* and Pasteur *(p.59)* were financed by their governments.

☑ Parliament gave Jenner *(p.43)* £10,000 for his research.

☑ In 1853, the government made smallpox vaccination compulsory.

☑ The Great Stink *(p.73)* of 1858 led the government to ask Bazalgette *(p.73)* to create a new London sewer system.

THE ROLE OF COMMUNICATION IN 18TH AND 19TH CENTURY MEDICINE

Communication played an important role in the development of medicine.

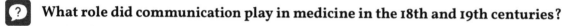

What role did communication play in medicine in the 18th and 19th centuries?

During the 18th and 19th centuries communication played a much greater role in medicine than before as new technology allowed ideas to be spread much more rapidly.

What are some examples of communication influencing medicine in the 18th and 19th centuries?

Here are some examples of the role that communication played.

☑ Lister brought French surgeon Pasteur's *(p.59)* germ theory *(p.59)* to Britain.

☑ News of Pasteur *(p.59)* and Koch's *(p.61)* vaccination discoveries were sent across Europe via electric telegraph.

☑ Aseptic surgical techniques were created because of the spread of Pasteur's *(p.59)* germ theory *(p.59)*.

THE ROLE OF RELIGION IN 18TH AND 19TH CENTURY MEDICINE

Religion played an important role in the development of medicine, however, during this period its role was diminishing.

What role did religion play in medicine in the 18th and 19th centuries?

Religion and superstition played a much smaller role in medicine during the 18th and 19th centuries as Britain was becoming more secular. However, some people did hold on to the old beliefs.

What are some examples of religion influencing medicine in the 18th and 19th century?

Before 1837, churches kept records of births, marriages and deaths.

DID YOU KNOW?

By the end of the 19th Century, the role of religion was pretty much non-existent!

Doctors still did not know what caused disease and some continued to believe in the pseudo-science of four humors (blood, yellow bile, black bile & phlegm), although belief in this theory declined during the 18th century.

THE ROLE OF WAR IN 18TH AND 19TH CENTURY MEDICINE

War played an important role in the development of medicine.

(?) What role did war play in medicine in the 18th and 19th centuries?

War played an important role in the development of medicine and surgery during the period as some wars led to new developments.

What are some examples of war influencing medicine in the 18th and 19th centuries?

Here are some examples of the role that war played.

- ☑ The French loss in the Franco-Prussian War in 1871 led to an increase in rivalry between Koch *(p.61)* and Pasteur *(p.59)*.
- ☑ When the Boer War broke out in 1899, thousands of volunteers were rejected as being too unfit to serve in the army. This led to government changes to public health.
- ☑ During the Crimean War in 1853 to 1856, Florence Nightingale *(p.57)* used to clean the hospital wards due to the fear of miasma, which ultimately led to reduced rates of infection.

DID YOU KNOW?

Many operations were performed during the war thanks to this.

Blood was first stored successfully during World War One. Doctors could now give blood transfusions to soldiers.

THE ROLE OF CHANCE IN 18TH AND 19TH CENTURY MEDICINE

Chance played an important role in the development of medicine.

(?) What role did chance play in medicine in the 18th and 19th centuries?

There were few new ideas about medicine discovered by chance during the 18th and 19th centuries but they were extremely significant.

What are some examples of chance influencing medicine in the 18th and 19th centuries?

Pasteur's *(p.59)* assistants accidentally injected a chicken with a weak strain of chicken cholera *(p.71)*. The chicken built up immunity.

DID YOU KNOW?

Chance allowed Pare to treat gunshot wounds.

Pare ran out of oil and was forced to use whatever was at hand to treat gunshot wounds. By chance he came up with a much improved solution which eased pain and healed wounds much more effectively.

MAGIC BULLETS

Targetting the germs that cause disease

What is a magic bullet?

A magic bullet is a chemical compound that will kill a specific germ without harming other cells.

Who discovered the magic bullet?

Paul Ehrlich worked with Robert Koch *(p.61)*, Emil von Behring and Sahachiro Hata. He is known for discovering the first 'magic bullet'.

How did Paul Ehrlich discover the first magic bullet?

There were 2 main stages in Ehrlich's discovery of magic bullets.

☑ In 1900, he suggested some chemicals might be able to kill specific germs.

☑ In 1909, Paul Ehrlich and Sahachiro Hata discovered the compound Salvarsan 606, which could kill the syphilis germ.

What was the first magic bullet?

The first magic bullet was Salvarsan 606, which was the 606th chemical compound tested by Ehrlich's team to treat syphilis.

What was the impact of the discovery of magic bullets?

Magic bullets had 3 key impacts on medicine.

☑ The discovery of magic bullets marked the birth of the modern pharmaceutical industry.

☑ In 1932, Gerhard Domagk discovered that blood poisoning could be cured using Prontosil.

☑ In 1935, French and Italian scientists at the Pasteur *(p.59)* Institute in Paris discovered bacteriostatic antibiotics based on how Prontosil affected the body. They had realised that bacteria in the body could not multiply because of Prontosil.

When were magic bullets developed?

The development of magic bullets took a number of years.

☑ The idea of magic bullets was first suggested by Paul Ehrlich in 1900.

☑ Salvarsan 606, the first magic bullet, was discovered in 1909.

DID YOU KNOW?

As well as discovering the cure for syphilis, Paul Ehrlich made a number of other significant medical discoveries.

He also made medical breakthroughs in haematology, chemotherapy and immunology.

X-RAYS

X-rays were an amazing discovery and have developed medicine tremendously.

How do x-rays work?

X-rays work by passing radiation through the body to produce images of bones, organs and tissue.

Who invented the X-ray machine?

The X-ray machine was invented by a German physicist named Wilhelm Roentgen.

When was the X-ray machine invented?

The X-ray machine was invented in 1895. The X-ray machine was very quickly put to use and was being used in London hospitals by 1896.

How could X-rays assist in medical treatment?

X-ray machines helped doctors in 4 key ways:

- ☑ They could show broken bones so they could be set properly.
- ☑ They could show where bullets or other foreign objects were lodged in the body.
- ☑ They could be used to identify the shadow on a lung that indicated tuberculosis.
- ☑ They could be used to show internal organs if the patient swallowed something that showed up on the X-ray.

DID YOU KNOW?

The 'x' in x-ray?

The 'x' in x-ray was used because by Roentgen because he didn't know the name of the new type of radiation that he found, so he labelled it 'x'.

KARL LANDSTEINER - BLOOD GROUPS

Blood transfusion was a very dangerous procedure, and the likelihood of survival was quite low.

What are blood transfusions?

Blood transfusions are when blood from another person is introduced into a patient's body.

When was the first blood transfusion?

The first blood transfusion was carried out in 1818.

Who discovered blood transfusion?

James Blundell carried out early blood transfusions, publishing his paper 'Experiments on the Transfusion of Blood by the Syringe' in 1818.

How were blood transfusions performed before the twentieth century?

Because blood clotted when it was removed from the body, early blood transfusions were directly donor-to-patient, and the donor had to be present.

Why were blood transfusions unsuccessful before 1901?

Only 50% of transfusions were successful before 1901.. There were 3 key problems:

- ✅ As blood could not be stored, transfusions involved the donor being directly attached to the recipient by a tube.
- ✅ It could often lead to death through infection.
- ✅ Patients' bodies rejected the new blood because they were given the wrong blood type, as blood groups had yet to be discovered.

How did the discovery of blood groups help in transfusions?

There were 3 key discoveries that led to more successful blood transfusions.

- ✅ In 1901, Karl Landsteiner discovered the A, B and O blood groups.
- ✅ In 1902, he discovered another blood group, AB.
- ✅ In 1907, it was discovered that type O blood was 'universal' and could safely be given to anyone.

What was the impact of blood transfusions?

Successful and safe blood transfusions helped with medical treatments in 3 main ways.

- ✅ They could be used in surgery.
- ✅ They could help patients suffering from blood disorders such as anaemia or leukaemia.
- ✅ They could be used to help people with liver problems, such as jaundice.

DID YOU KNOW?

Karl Landsteiner developed the modern system of classification of blood groups.

Landsteiner has an impressive list of achievements and his discoveries go down as some of the most important findings in medical history. In 1930, years after his discovery, he was awarded the Nobel Prize for his work on blood groups.

IMPACT OF WAR - TREATMENTS

Throughout history, war has often brought about much-needed medical and technological advances.

What medical treatments did they use in the First World War?

Doctors developed new treatments for the illnesses and injuries that were caused by the fighting and by the conditions in the trenches.

What medical treatments for wounded limbs were developed during the First World War?

There were many injuries to arms and legs in the First World War - 240,000 soldiers lost limbs through amputation. New techniques were developed as a result:

- ✅ The Thomas splint was used to keep injured legs still, while soldiers were being transported from the front.
- ✅ Lighter and more mobile prosthetic limbs were developed for amputees.

Which medical treatments were used to treat gas injuries in the First World War?

Around 186,000 British soldiers on the Western Front were affected by gas injuries, but only around 2.6% of them died. There were different treatments for different gas injuries:

- ☑ Soldiers affected by chlorine and phosgene gas needed oxygen, and were kept in hospital for up to two months.
- ☑ Mobile shower units were set up for soldiers affected by mustard gas, as they had to wash with soap and water to prevent burns. Their eyes also needed bathing as soon as possible.

Which medical treatments were used to fight infections in the First World War?

During the First World War, doctors developed a number of ways to prevent wounds becoming infected in the dirty conditions of the Western Front:

- ☑ Soldiers were given anti-tetanus serum to protect against tetanus.
- ☑ Wounds were washed in carbolic *(p.67)* lotion, an antiseptic *(p.67)* solution. Once the wounds were closed, they were wrapped in bandages soaked in carbolic acid *(p.67)*.
- ☑ Amputations were carried out to prevent life-threatening infections spreading through the bodies of the injured.
- ☑ Wound excision, or debridement, involved cutting dead tissue away from a wound to prevent infection.
- ☑ The Carrel-Dakin method was a system of tubes that ensured a constant supply of sterilised salt solution to a wound.

What new medical treatments were developed in the First World War?

Doctors developed several new medical techniques and practices to deal with injuries in the First World War. These included:

- ☑ The use of mobile X-ray *(p.79)* machines.
- ☑ Blood transfusions and blood banks.
- ☑ Brain surgery *(p.82)*.
- ☑ Plastic surgery *(p.81)*.

DID YOU KNOW?

Wartime doctors and surgeons didn't know how to treat all wounds caused by war.

Some wounds caused by war were not always visible. We now know that psychological trauma caused by war is known as post-traumatic stress disorder (PTSD). However, during the First World War it was called 'shellshock'. Soldiers would have panic attacks or be unable to speak or move. Some doctors refused to treat this and saw these men as weak. By the end of the First World War there so many cases that it became officially recognised, and occasionally treated by the use of a very basic form of psychotherapy.

PLASTIC SURGERY IN THE FIRST WORLD WAR

During the First World War a New Zealand-born, London-based army doctor made strides in what we now call plastic surgery.

What reasons were there for the development of plastic surgery in the First World War?

Some soldiers suffered horrific, disfiguring facial wounds. They often suffered psychological problems as a result of their appearance.

What treatment was available to disfigured soldiers at the start of WWI?

At the beginning of the war, the only solution was a mask made of tin.

Who was responsible for developing plastic surgery in the First World War?

Sir Harold Gillies, an ear, nose and throat surgeon from New Zealand, pioneered several new techniques to improve the appearance of facial wounds.

What techniques did plastic surgeons use in the First World War?

The plastic surgeons of the First World War developed a number of new techniques. These included:

- ☑ Pedicle tubes that were used to keep the blood flowing to skin grafts, to prevent the body from rejecting them.
- ☑ Bone and cartilage were used to make new facial features for soldiers who had suffered facial damage.

Where was plastic surgery developed in the First World War?

Queen's Hospital in Sidcup, Kent, was set up to care for soldiers with facial wounds. It was run by Sir Harold Gillies.

How many soldiers underwent plastic surgery in the First World War?

By the end of the war, over 12,000 patients had undergone plastic surgery.

DID YOU KNOW?

Gillies helped treat over 5,000 soldiers.

Gillies was one the first doctors to realise the mental strain severe facial wounds could have on a soldier. In 1917 Queen's Hospital in Kent opened and had over 1,000 beds by 1921. By 1921 Gillies and his team had treated over 5,000 wounded soldiers by 1921.

BRAIN SURGERY IN THE FIRST WORLD WAR

The use of brain surgery greatly advanced because of the types of injuries that occured on the battlefield.

What was the reason for the development of neurosurgery during the First World War?

The number of soldiers receiving brain injuries led to the development of neurosurgery thoughout the war.

What were the difficulties with neurosurgery during the First World War?

There were 2 main difficulties with neurosurgery in 1914:

- ☑ Head wounds affecting the brain were often fatal, because unconscious patients were difficult to move through the chain *(p.88)* of evacuation.
- ☑ Surgeons had little experience of neurosurgery.

Who developed neurosurgery during the First World War?

American neurosurgeon Harvey *(p.41)* Cushing used new techniques to treat brain injuries.

How was neurosurgery used to treat brain injuries in the First World War?

Two main methods were developed to deal with brain injuries:

☑ Magnets were used to remove metal fragments from the brain.

☑ Local anaesthetic *(p.64)* was used because it reduced swelling to the brain. General anaesthetic was found to increase swelling and therefore made brain surgery more dangerous.

What were the results of Harvey Cushing's work on neurosurgery during the First World War?

Cushing's techniques improved the survival rate from brain surgery, from an average of 50% to 71%.

How did the Brodie helmet reduce the need for neurosurgery in the First World War?

In 1915, the Brodie helmet was introduced to help prevent head injuries. It was made from steel and had a strap to keep it on the soldier's head. It is estimated that it reduced the fatality of head wounds by 80%.

DID YOU KNOW?

One of the fathers of neurology died on the battlefield.

Sir Victor Horsley, who discovered useful techniques to make brain surgery quicker and faster, died of heatstroke on the battlefield while serving as a field surgeon for the British army in Mesopotamia during the First World War.

IMPACT OF WAR: X-RAYS

X-rays at this time were used in a similar way to which they're used now.

Were X-rays used in the First World War?

X-rays were first invented in 1895, but they were put to more common use during the First World War.

How were X-rays used in the First World War?

There were 2 main uses of X-rays in the First World War:

☑ Before surgeons operated on patients with bullet and shrapnel injuries, two X-rays were taken of the wounds, so the surgeons knew exactly where the pieces were located.

☑ British Base Hospitals, and some Casualty Clearing Stations, had large X-ray *(p.79)* machines.

What were the disadvantages of X-ray machines during the First World War?

The use of X-rays in the First World War was problematic, particularly with the mobile units. There were 5 main problems.

☑ The radiation from X-ray *(p.79)* machines could be harmful and cause burns.

☑ Pictures from mobile X-ray *(p.79)* machines were of poorer quality than those from the larger static machines. They were, however, usually good enough for the surgeons to work from.

☑ Soldiers had to remain still for a few minutes while the X-ray *(p.79)* was taken, even if they were in pain.

☑ The tubes of the X-ray *(p.79)* machine were fragile, and became too hot if the machine was used for more than an hour at a time.

☑ X-rays could only identify objects such as bullets and shrapnel. They could not identify fragments of clothing or soil in a wound.

IMPACT OF WAR - THE SECOND WORLD WAR

In the Second World War, doctors, surgeons and scientists had to work tirelessly to create new medicines and techniques.

How did the Second World War change medicine?

The Second World War and its resulting injuries drove further developments in the world of medicine. There were particular advances in the areas of blood transfusions and skin grafts.

Who were the pioneering surgeons of the Second World War medicine?

Some famous surgeons in the Second World War were a British neurosurgeon called Wylie McKissock, an American heart surgeon named Dwight Harken, and Archibald McIndoe, a plastic surgeon from New Zealand.

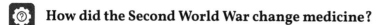

PLASTIC SURGERY IN THE SECOND WORLD WAR

Injuries left some soldiers unrecognisable, and plastic surgery was needed to try to reconstruct their faces.

What was the reason for plastic surgery developing during the Second World War?

The increased use of machinery such as aircraft and tanks meant that burn injuries were more common. Surgeons therefore developed new methods to treat them effectively.

What better methods of plastic surgery were developed to treat burns victims in WW2?

Surgeons developed new and better methods of plastic surgery *(p.81)* to treat burns victims:

☑ Saline, instead of chemicals, was used to treat burns, which improved movement in the area when the burn had healed.

- ☑ The war led to new advances in skin graft methods by transfering healthy skin to an injured area.
- ☑ Penicillin *(p.87)* was used to prevent infection when treating burns victims.

DID YOU KNOW?

A New Zealand doctor reconstructed soldiers' damaged faces.

Archibald McIndoe, a New Zealand doctor who had trained and worked in Britain, used new drugs such as penicillin to reduce the chance of infections when treating pilots who had suffered terrible facial injuries. His work came to be respected all over the world

---

PSYCHOLOGICAL TREATMENT IN THE SECOND WORLD WAR

Psychological problems during war time was nothing new. The Second World War saw more awareness or the psychological impact of warfare on soldiers.

How did they treat PTSD in the Second World War?

In the Second World War, psychological problems were often known as battle fatigue. Understanding of the psychological impact of warfare had improved by the Second World War, and 18 psychiatric hospitals were set up in peaceful surroundings.

DID YOU KNOW?

The psychological impacts weren't always visible.

When soldiers came home from the Second World War their wounds were not always visible. Psychological problems from the Second World War could affect a soldier for the rest of their lives.

BLOOD TRANSFUSIONS IN THE SECOND WORLD WAR

By the Second World War, blood transfusion technology and knowledge had progressed a great deal. More people felt the need to donate their blood, especially in times of war.

What developments were there in blood transfusions in the Second World War?

During the Second World War, blood transfusion *(p.79)* became more common and more effective due to a number of new developments.

What were the key developments in blood transfusion during the Second World War?

There were 4 key developments in blood transfusions:

- ☑ Blood donations became more common. Around 700,000 people gave blood during the Second World War.
- ☑ There were better facilities for storing blood, such as the Army Blood Supply Depot located in Bristol.
- ☑ Doctors began to use blood plasma for transfusions and developed a dried plasma package which was easier to store and transport.

☑ In 1939, the discovery of the rhesus blood group, and work on the tetanus vaccination, meant blood transfusions became safer.

DID YOU KNOW?

Dr. Charles Drew saved thousands of lives with his discoveries.

Charles Drew, an African-American surgeon and researcher discovered techniques to help preserve blood-plasma. He was the first African-American to gain success in this field and the first to be given a doctor of science degree. He was asked to help facilitate the 'Blood For Britain' campaign and was then asked to organise a similar campaign in the USA. He was appalled that donated blood was divided into different racial groups and resigned from the project.

ALEXANDER FLEMING

Discovering penicillin

👤 Who was Alexander Fleming?

Sir Alexander Fleming was a Scottish scientist, who discovered the antibiotic *(p.87)* properties of penicillin in 1928.

What was Alexander Fleming's background?

Alexander Fleming had been an army doctor in the First World War, where he saw many men die of infection caused by the staphylococcus bacteria and septicaemia.

What were Fleming's early discoveries?

In 1922, Fleming's research identified that an enzyme called lysozyme, found in human tears, killed certain harmless bacteria.

How did Fleming discover penicillin?

In 1928, Fleming accidentally left some staphylococcus bacteria on a culture plate in his lab. After two weeks he noticed that penicillium notatum (a green mould) had stopped the bacteria from growing.

Where did Fleming publish his findings?

In 1929, Fleming published his findings about penicillin *(p.87)* in the 'British Journal of Experimental Pathology'.

What problems did Fleming face?

Fleming was unable to develop his research into penicillin *(p.87)* after 1929 for 3 key reasons:

☑ It was difficult to grow enough penicillium (the fungus) for effective research.

☑ Penicillin *(p.87)* appeared to take time to have an effect, and its effectiveness was limited when mixed with blood.

☑ Fleming was unable to get funding for more research.

DID YOU KNOW?

Fleming studied a wide range of sciences.

He was a biologist, physician, microbiologist and pharmacologist.

Quizzes, amazing exam preparation tools and more at GCSEHistory.com

PENICILLIN AND ANTIBIOTICS

Developing the use of antibiotics

What is penicillin?

Penicillin was the first antibiotic to be discovered, and was originally derived from common penicillium mould.

What type of medicine is penicillin?

Antibiotics are microbes that can kill the germs that cause diseases.

How did people use penicillin before it was discovered?

In the Middle Ages, people used mouldy bread to treat infection in a wound, and in 1871 Joseph Lister used it to treat a patient.

When was penicillin discovered?

Penicillin was discovered in 1928.

What bacteria did penicillin treat?

The staphylococcus bacteria is a germ that causes many infections.

Who developed Fleming's research on penicillin?

In 1939, Howard Florey *(p.88)* and Ernst Chain *(p.88)* at Oxford University began to look into Fleming's *(p.86)* discoveries. Helped by Norman Heatley, they conducted more tests.

How did Florey and Chain test penicillin?

Florey *(p.88)* and Chain *(p.88)* tested penicillin in 3 stages although they found it difficult to produce enough to be effective:

- ☑ In 1940, their first tests were on mice, which recovered from streptococci with penicillin.
- ☑ In 1941, their first human subject was a policeman with septicaemia. The penicillin helped, but there was not enough to cure him and he died.
- ☑ They developed penicillin to treat children, as a smaller dose was needed.

Who funded the development of penicillin?

Americans were initially responsible for funding the large-scale production of penicillin. Florey *(p.88)* travelled to the U.S. to seek help from the American pharmaceutical industry. They convinced four drug companies to invest.

Why was it possible to mass-produce penicillin?

Penicillin could be mass-produced for 5 key reasons:

- ☑ Individuals such as Fleming *(p.86)*, Florey *(p.88)* and Chain *(p.88)* were actively looking for solutions to infections. Florey's decision not to patent their findings made penicillin affordable.
- ☑ The development of techniques to grow and observe germs helped scientists discover antibiotics.
- ☑ The First World War showed the impact that infections could have in wartime, while the Second World War gave governments the incentive to find and fund solutions.
- ☑ The technological advance of mass production techniques made it easier to make penicillin.
- ☑ The American government funded Florey's *(p.88)* research for five years. Institutions such as governments funded and encouraged the production of penicillin.

What is the impact of penicillin?

Penicillin is estimated to have saved 200 million lives since its development.

How has penicillin been developed further?

A synthetic (chemical) version of penicillin was created in 1955.

Who got the Nobel Prize for penicillin?

In 1945, Fleming *(p.86)*, Florey *(p.88)* and Chain *(p.88)* were jointly awarded the Nobel Prize for Medicine for their work on penicillin.

Why are scientists constantly researching new antibiotics?

Scientists are constantly working on researching and finding new antibiotics. This is because of the problem of the development of penicillin-resistant bacteria.

DID YOU KNOW?

In the early stages of their research, Florey and Chain struggled to grow enough penicillin to treat a human.

Because there was so little penicillin in the mould, they grew mould on as many available surfaces as they could - including milk bottles, tea trays and bedpans. Later, Americans would use gigantic beer vats to produce the mould.

HOWARD FLOREY

Australian pathologist who developed research into penicillin

Who was Howard Florey?

Howard Florey was an Australian scientist who worked with Ernst Chain *(p.88)* to further research the potential of penicillin *(p.87)*.

ERNST CHAIN

German biochemist who developed research into penicillin

Who was Ernst Chain?

Ernst Chain was a German scientist who worked with Howard Florey *(p.88)* to develop tests on penicillin *(p.87)*.

GENETIC UNDERSTANDING

The discovery of DNA has helped saved many lives

What is DNA?

DNA carries the information needed to develop the characteristics of any living organism. It is the building block of human cells and is responsible for passing on genetic characteristics to children.

Where was DNA discovered?

DNA was discovered at Cambridge University.

What does DNA stand for?

DNA stands for Deoxyribonucleic Acid.

How was DNA discovered?

DNA had already been discovered by scientists in the late 1800s, but in 1963 scientists James Watson and Francis Crick discovered its double helix structure which allowed later scientists to understand genetic diseases.

How did scientists learn about DNA?

The Human Genome Project *(p.89)* was set up in 1990 to better understand human DNA. Teams of scientists mapped all the genes in DNA to understand the effect each one had on the body.

DID YOU KNOW?

It was a woman who discovered the structure of DNA.

It was Rosalind Franklin who, through photo development, discovered that DNA has a double helix structure; this was called Photograph 51. Her colleague Maurice Wilkins showed this photo to James Watson who published the findings in a scientific paper without crediting Franklin.

THE HUMAN GENOME PROJECT

The Human Genome Project was a massive breakthrough in understanding in genetics.

What was the Human Genome Project?

The Human Genome Project involved an international team of scientists working together to decode the human genome . As a result of their efforts, there is now a 'genetic blueprint' for human beings.

When was the Human Genome Project?

The Human Genome Project lasted from 1990 to 2003. It finished two years ahead of schedule.

Who set up the Human Genome Project?

James Watson set up the Human Genome Project.

How has the Human Genome Project been used to treat illness and disease?

Once DNA *(p.89)* had been mapped, scientists could use the information to treat people suffering from genetic diseases. Examples include:

- ☑ A gene was identified that is sometimes present in breast cancer sufferers. People can now be tested to see whether they carry that gene.
- ☑ It has been used to reverse mutations that cause blindness.
- ☑ It has been used to make some cells resistant to HIV (the virus that causes AIDS).

DID YOU KNOW?

A human genome is huge!

Written out it would be around 5,592 miles long! It would fill up around 5,000 books.

ALTERNATIVE TREATMENTS

We know that not all diseases have cures, even with the advancement of medicine. Some have sought alternative treatments.

What is alternative medicine?

Alternative medicine is any other way of treating an illness that doesn't rely on scientific, peer-reviewed, proven and doctor-dispensed medicine.

Why do people use alternative medicines?

People use this because there are still no cures for certain syndromes such as AIDS or some types of cancer so they turn to alternative ways of improving their health.

How does alternative medicine work?

Many alternative treatments are intended to consider the patient as a whole, instead of using mainstream medicines to target a specific problem or part of the body.

How popular is alternative medicine?

Since the 1980s, alternative treatments have become popular. Approximately, 1 in 5 people in Britain have used alternative medicines.

How are prevention methods used as alternative medicine?

There has been more focus on preventing illnesses rather than curing them. This is done through living healthy lifestyles, regularly exercising, and avoiding sugary, fatty foods.

What are some examples of alternative medicines?

There are four examples of alternative medicines used in Britain.

- ☑ Aromatherapy *(p.91)*.
- ☑ Acupuncture *(p.92)*.
- ☑ Hypnotherapy *(p.91)*.

☑ Homeopathy *(p.92)*.

 **Why do some people oppose alternative treatments?**

People oppose alternative treatments for different reasons:

☑ There is a lack of regulation. Anyone is able to practise alternative medicine without formal qualifications.

☑ There is a lack of scientfic proof that it works. Doctors in particular often dismiss it as 'quackery *(p.45)*'.

DID YOU KNOW?

Some alternative medicines are available on the NHS.

Although alternative medicines come at a cost some are available through the NHS, such as acupuncture and homeopathy.

AROMATHERAPY

Aromatherapy is often used to help people to relax and heal and is mostly from natural substances.

? **What is aromatherapy?**

This is the use of essential oils from flowers and fruits which are inhaled or massaged into the skin.

What is the effect of aromatherapy?

It is supposed to stimulate certain areas of the brain and promote healing.

DID YOU KNOW?

The first time the world 'aromatherapy' was used was in France.

The term was first found in the book 'Aromathérapie: Les Huiles Essentielles, Hormones Végétales' by René-Maurice Gattefossé. Gattefossé had burnt his hand very severely and said the use of lavender oil helped heal the wound.

HYPNOTHERAPY

Hypnotherapy has been used more and more in recent years.

? **What is hypnotherapy?**

Hypnotherapy is where a patient is hypnotised.

What is the effect of hypnotherapy?

It is supposed to totally relax the patient's body and make them think positively to bring about the change they need.

HOMEOPATHY

Another type of alternative medicine is homeopathy, it is hoped that it will help stimulates patients natural defences.

What is homeopathy?

Homeopathy is where a patient takes a medicine that produces symptoms similar to the illness they are suffering from.

What is the effect of homeopathy?

It is supposed to stimulate the patient's natural defences and helps them fight off the symptoms. It has been effective in treating conditions such as eczema and hay fever.

ACUPUNCTURE

Acupuncture has become incredibly popular and is used to treat many types of illnesses.

What is acupuncture?

This is where needles are placed at key points around the body. These points are supposedly linked with particular illnesses.

What is the effect of acupuncture?

The needles are supposed to release blocked energy and help it to flow again. It also relieves pain.

LIBERAL REFORMS

Laissez-faire ideas were being replaced with more a hands-on approach to healthcare.

What was the purpose of the Liberal reforms from 1906?

After the Liberal Party won the 1906 general election by a landslide, they began to introduce reforms to tackle poverty. Poverty was the cause of many health problems in British society.

Who did the Liberal reforms try to help?

The Liberal reforms aimed to help the most vulnerable members of society:

- ☑ The young.
- ☑ The old.
- ☑ The sick.
- ☑ The unemployed.

Why did the Liberal Party introduce reforms after 1906?

By 1906, there were 4 main factors which contributed to people realising that poverty was a very real problem in Britain:

- ☑ Social studies by Rowntree and Booth between 1891 and 1903, showed that many people lived below the poverty line, suffering from malnutrition and poor health.
- ☑ Britain needed a strong, healthy army to defend its empire. However, more than a third of recruits for the Boer War (1899-1902) were unfit as a result of poverty.
- ☑ People had to pay to see a doctor. Some doctors had 'sick clubs', where people paid an amount each week to cover their costs, but many people couldn't afford medical care.
- ☑ The Industrial Revolution had reduced the health of the people as it had created poor living conditions for the working classes. This had increased disease.

How did the Liberal reforms help children?

The Liberals introduced 3 main laws, between 1906 and 1908, to reduce poverty and ill-health in children:

- ☑ The Free School Meals Act of 1906 allowed local authorities to provide free school meals from local taxes, although many chose not to.
- ☑ In 1907, free medical inspections were introduced in schools.
- ☑ In 1908, the Children's Act made it illegal to neglect children, or to sell them alcohol or tobacco.

How did the Liberal reforms help the elderly?

In 1908, an 'old age pension' of five shillings a week was introduced for poor people over the age of 70.

How did the Liberal reforms help the unemployed?

In 1909, Labour Exchanges were developed to help the unemployed look for work. In 1911, the National Insurance Act provided them with unemployment payments.

 How did the National Insurance Act, introduced under the Liberal reforms, help workers?

The National Insurance Act of 1911 provided a number of benefits to workers:

- ☑ It provided sick pay to ill workers, and allowed them to access free medical treatment.
- ☑ It paid money to workers without jobs for up to 15 weeks, and prevented them falling into poverty.
- ☑ It was paid for by contributions from employers, the government, and the workers themselves.

DID YOU KNOW?

School dinners weren't that tasty!

An average school menu for the week would include the basic staples - meat, vegetables, various puddings and, on Friday, a fish dish. Some things haven't changed!

BEVERIDGE REPORT

William Beveridge put together 'The Beveridge Report', which would eventually help form the Welfare State.

 Who was William Beveridge?

William Beveridge was a government minister, who wrote a report about rebuilding Britain after the Second World War.

 When was the Beveridge Report published?

William Beveridge published The Beveridge Report in 1942.

 What problems in society did Beveridge suggest the government should tackle?

The Beveridge Report suggested the government had a role to play in tackling the 5 'giant evils' of British society:

- ☑ Want (poverty).
- ☑ Disease.
- ☑ Ignorance (lack of education).
- ☑ Squalor (unhygienic living conditions).
- ☑ Idleness (unemployment).

 What was the significance of the Beveridge Report?

The Beveridge Report became very famous, and raised people's hopes that the government would do more to build a healthier society after the Second World War. It formed the basis of the welfare state. *(p.95)*

 How did the governement respond to the Beveridge Report?

The government took 5 key measures to fix the 5 'giant evils'.

- ✅ The government introduced a range of benefits. For example a weekly family allowance, paid to the mother.
- ✅ The NHS *(p.96)* was created.
- ✅ The Clean Air Acts (1952 & 1956) aimed to reduce pollution in towns and cities.
- ✅ The government embarked on a slum clearance programme in the 1960s. They were replaced by council housing with modern conveniences such as central heating.
- ✅ New towns, such as Milton Keynes, were built from scratch with more space and better public facilities like parks.

DID YOU KNOW?

William Beveridge paved the way for a new society.

The Beveridge report was seen as radical when it was published. Beveridge's ideas were profound and somewhat unheard of. However, by 1943, around 86 percent of Britons were in favour of the ideas proposed in the report. Many have argued that it achieved a social revolution.

WELFARE STATE

'From the cradle to the grave'.

What was the purpose of the Welfare State?

After the Second World War, British Prime Minister Clement Attlee and his Labour government set up the welfare state to provide care for everyone, 'from the cradle to the grave'.

How did the Second World War contribute to the creation of the Welfare State?

The Second World War helped to bring about the creation of the Welfare State in 3 key ways.

- ✅ The war forced Britain to deal with large numbers of injuries.
- ✅ The war expanded the role of the government in health, with the Emergency Medical Service.
- ✅ People were shocked at the state of the hygiene and health of some of the evacuees.

What new measures did the Labour government introduce under the Welfare State?

The Labour government introduced 3 main reforms after 1945 that affected health.

- ✅ The New Towns Act of 1946 was introduced, to plan new towns.
- ✅ The National Insurance Act of 1946 provided better unemployment and sick pay, maternity benefits, and improved old age pensions.
- ✅ The National Health Service *(p.96)* was launched in 1948, which provided free healthcare at the point of delivery and was paid for by taxes.

DID YOU KNOW?

The Welfare State was mostly supported, but some people objected to it.

As with the NHS, the Welfare State was opposed by some groups of people, especially on the right-wing of politics. Some were afraid that taxes would increase and some thought that it would discourage people from looking for jobs and would encourage the poor to 'live off the state'.

NHS

In 1948, many had never seen a medical professional before as it was very costly - the NHS gave everyone a chance to receive medical care.

What was the NHS?

The National Health Service (NHS) was set up to provide free healthcare to patients at the point of delivery.

Who was responsible for establishing the NHS?

Aneurin Bevan was a Labour Minister for Health from Wales, who was responsible for setting up the NHS.

Why was the NHS introduced?

By the end of the Second World War, changes to society meant that the idea of a public health service was much more popular, for 5 key reasons.

☑ Many children were evacuated to the country during the Second World War. People were horrified by the poverty that they saw.

☑ By the mid-twentieth century, people had become more used to the idea of the government playing a role in people's lives.

☑ Advances in medicine meant that there were more ways to help the sick.

☑ The Second World War had already forced the government to organise, and take more control of, hospitals and medical services.

☑ The Beveridge *(p.94)* Report of 1942 inspired the creation of the NHS.

When did the NHS begin?

The NHS was founded on 5th July, 1948.

Who opposed the creation of the NHS?

There were 2 main areas of opposition to the creation of the NHS.

☑ Some doctors opposed the introduction of the NHS because it reduced their income from private patients. Bevan promised they could continue to work privately, as well as receiving a salary from the government.

☑ Many Conservatives disliked the NHS because of the burden on the taxpayer, but it was too popular with the general public to be abolished.

How was the NHS organised?

The NHS was organised in the following ways:

☑ Hospitals were controlled by 14 regional boards, but were made part of a single system.

☑ Doctors, as well as dentists, pharmacists and opticians, had individual contracts with the NHS.

☑ GPs played an important role in providing primary health care, by diagnosing and treating patients, by referring them to hospital where necessary, or writing prescriptions for medicine.

☑ Local health authorities had responsibility for vaccination programmes, maternal and child welfare, health visitors, and school dental services. They were led by a medical officer.

What services does the NHS provide?

The NHS provides services through medical treatment, hospitals, specialist healthcare professionals, preventative healthcare, and care for the vulnerable.

☑ The NHS provides treatment for illness and injury, including surgery, blood transfusions and medication.

- The NHS runs hospitals, provides ambulance services to transport patients to them, and accident and emergency care.
- The NHS provides access to healthcare professionals and services such as GPs, mental health services, dental treatment, and opticians.
- The NHS works to prevent illness to cut down on the cost of treatment. This includes campaigns to encourage healthier lifestyles, vaccinations, and diagnostic screening.
- The NHS provides care for the vulnerable, such as the elderly and disabled. Maternity care and health visitors are provided for mothers and new babies.

In what ways has the NHS been successful?

The NHS has been successful in improving healthcare in Britain in 6 main ways.

- The NHS has improved hospitals and healthcare facilities.
- The NHS has led to a fall in child mortality rates.
- The NHS has implemented a national vaccination scheme, eradicating many diseases.
- The NHS provides free healthcare for all, regardless of their ability to pay.
- The NHS has raised life expectancy.
- The NHS lowers treatment costs by promoting preventive health care.

How much did the NHS cost?

The NHS was paid for by National Insurance contributions and taxes. In 1948, it cost £12.9 billion.

How much did the NHS raise life expectancy?

In 1930, on average, men lived until the age of 58 and women until 62. By 1950, this had increased to 66 for men and 70 for women.

What happened to the NHS in the 1960s?

During the 1960s, the government built more hospitals across the country, and introduced a GP's charter in 1966, which improved standards in care.

DID YOU KNOW?

The NHS was the first of its kind!

When the NHS was established in July, 1948 it was the first time in history that there had been an organised healthcare system that was free on point of service. Many other countries have since used the NHS model for their own healthcare systems.

THE CONTRIBUTION OF NEW TECHNOLOGY TO MODERN MEDICINE

Developments in technology have opened up new possibilities in the treatment of illness, disease and surgery.

? ### What is new technology used for in the development of medicine?

As technology advances in the modern world there is now a wide range of machines and technologies used to diagnose, monitor and treat patients.

What are the different types of new technology in medicine used for?

New technology is used in a variety of ways in modern medicine.

- ☑ Various monitors can be used to check a patient's blood pressure, oxygen levels, and heart rate.
- ☑ During the 1990s, increased use of keyhole surgery - using endoscopes - allowed surgeons to carry out complex surgery with minimal trauma to patients and a reduced risk of infection. This can now be done using robotics, making incisions even smaller.
- ☑ MRI scanning and CT scanning create 3D images of the skeleton and soft tissue inside the body. This helps doctors diagnose and treat patients more accurately.
- ☑ In-vitro fertilisation, or IVF, was discovered in the 1970s as a way to help those with fertility issues have children.
- ☑ Dialysis machines are used to treat the blood of patients with kidney failure.
- ☑ Prosthetic limbs are used to replace lost body parts: for example, for soldiers in war.
- ☑ Lasers and robotics can be used for precision in surgery.
- ☑ Surgeons now have the ability to transplant organs through surgery. The first kidney was transplanted in 1956, between identical twins. The first lungs were transplanted in 1963, and the first heart in 1967.

DID YOU KNOW?

In 2010 doctors performed the first ever full face transplant.

After a Spanish farmer accidentally shot himself in the face, doctors were able to replace his face with that of a donor, including the jaw and teeth.

THE ROLE OF THE INDIVIDUAL IN MODERN MEDICINE

Without the brilliance of individuals, medicine would not have progressed.

? ### What role did the individual play in medicine in modern times?

The individual played a smaller role within medicine compared to the 19th century, especially after the Second World War. From then, large corporations used teams of scientists, rather than individuals, to make new discoveries.

What are some examples of individuals influencing medicine in modern times?

Here are 3 key examples of the role that the individual played.

- ☑ Aneurin Bevan led the creation of the NHS *(p.96)* in 1948.
- ☑ Charles Booth and Seebohm Rowntree wrote reports on British poverty and poor health.
- ☑ Fleming *(p.86)* discovered penicillin *(p.87)*.

THE ROLE OF SCIENCE AND TECHNOLOGY IN MODERN MEDICINE

Science and technology played an important role in the development of medicine, it has come a long way since the Middle Ages.

What role did science and technology play in medicine in modern times?

Science and technology advanced greatly in this period so medicine and surgery progressed rapidly. It was very important.

What are some examples of science and technology influencing medicine in modern times?

Here are 3 key examples of the role that the science and technology played.

- ✅ First open-heart surgery in 1950 and heart transplant in 1967.
- ✅ First vaccine to target a kind of cancer in 2006.
- ✅ MRI scanning used from 1987 to discover tumours.

THE ROLE OF THE GOVERNMENT IN MODERN MEDICINE

Governments play a major role in health care financing by mobilizing the necessary resources through public budgets and other contributive mechanisms.

What role did the government play in medicine in modern times?

During the 20th century the government introduced a wide range of new laws to improve public health. It became extremely significant.

What are some examples of the government influencing medicine in modern times?

Here are 4 main examples of the role that the government played.

- ☑ The UK and US governments funded research into penicillin *(p.87)* during the Second World War.
- ☑ The Liberal government began reforming public health from 1906.
- ☑ Labour established the NHS *(p.96)* in 1948.
- ☑ The government now funds breast and cervical cancer screening programmes.

DID YOU KNOW?

Many Government laws have been passed to keep the public safe.

Government regulation plays a major role in the health care industry and health care insurance coverage. Various regulatory bodies protect the public from a number of health risks and provide numerous programs for public health and welfare.

THE ROLE OF COMMUNICATION IN MODERN MEDICINE

Communication played an important role in the development of medicine.

 ### What role did communication play in medicine in modern times?

During the 20th century communication played a much greater role in medicine than before as new technology allowed ideas to be spread much more rapidly.

 ### What are some examples of communication influencing medicine in modern times?

Here are some examples of the role that communication played.

- ☑ TV and radio advertisements have made more people than ever before aware of the risks of smoking and drinking.
- ☑ The internet allows scientists to share their ideas widely and quickly.

DID YOU KNOW?

A report released in 2016 revealed that around 2,000 patient deaths could have been avoided if only doctors and nurses possessed enough knowledge on how to communicate better.

THE ROLE OF WAR IN MODERN MEDICINE

Conflicts have always enabled medical practionners to come up with revised methods to cure patients more safely and efficiently.

What role did war play in medicine in modern times?

War was a very important factor in the development of medicine and surgery, as large-scale wars in the 20th century led to a range of new discoveries.

What are some examples of war influencing medicine in modern times?

Here are some examples of the role that war played.

- ✅ Fleming *(p.86)* was sent to study the treatment of wounded soldiers during the First World War.
- ✅ Doctors realised that war can cause mental illnesses like PTSD.
- ✅ Plastic surgery *(p.81)* and prosthetics developed during the World Wars.

DID YOU KNOW?

Many key developments in healthcare have their origins in the battlefield where the treatment of injured troops has led to innovations throughout history which continue today

---

THE ROLE OF CHANCE IN MODERN MEDICINE

In the development of medicine there have been several occasions where breakthroughs have happened as a result of chance.

What role did chance play in medicine in the modern times?

There were few new ideas about medicine discovered by chance during the 20th century but they were extremely significant.

What are some examples of chance influencing medicine in modern times?

Fleming *(p.86)* discovered the uses of penicillin *(p.87)* by accident when he left the staphylococcus germ while he went on holiday.

DID YOU KNOW?

Pasteur and his meeting with a boy bitten by a dog - developed the rabies vaccination in 1885

GLOSSARY

A

Abolish, Abolished - to stop something, or get rid of it.

Alchemy - the study of the properties of different matter and subsequent attempts to transform, create or combine them to make something else. Often used in relation to turning something into gold.

Amputate, Amputation - to surgically remove a limb from someone's body.

Anaesthetic - a drug used in surgery to remove pain by causing a temporary loss of sensation or awareness.

Anatomist - someone who studies and conducts research on the human body.

Anatomy - the study of how the body is made up internally, what it looks like, how it is structured and how the different parts are positioned.

Antibiotics - microbes that can kill germs that cause diseases.

Antiseptic - a substance that kills harmful bacteria to prevent infection.

Apothecaries, Apothecary - a non-medically trained person who concocted remedies from herbs.

Aseptic - an absence of germs and harmful bacteria; surgically sterile.

Astrologists - one who studies astrology

Astrology - the study of the alignment of the planets and stars.

B

Bacteria, Bacterium - a microorganism that causes diseases.

Bacteriology - the study of bacteria.

Barber surgeon - someone who could cut and shave hair, and who also carried out basic surgery such as bloodletting.

Bile, Black bile - one of the four 'humours' in medieval medicine. A black substance observed in excrement and vomit, it probably constituted clotted blood.

Blood group - refers to the type of blood someone has and used to distinguish between different types for blood transfusions.

Blood transfusion - the process of giving a patient blood from a donor.

Bloodletting - the process of removing blood from the body, thought to be a way of preventing or curing certain illnesses and diseases.

Buboes - painful swellings in the neck, armpit and groin areas that were a symptom of bubonic plague.

C

Campaign - a political movement to get something changed; in military terms, it refers to a series of operations to achieve a goal.

Catgut - a material made from the dried, twisted intestines of sheep or horses and used as a ligature.

Catholic - a Christian who belongs to the Roman Catholic Church.

Cauterise - to burn the flesh of a wound to stop it bleeding.

Cesspit - a hole which has been dug to store sewage and waste.

Charter - a legal written grant, issued by a monarch or country's legislative power, permitting certain rights or privileges.

Choler - pus or stomach acid found in vomit. It was one of the four 'humours' in medieval medicine.

Circulation, Circulatory - the movement of blood around the body pumped by the heart.

Civil servant - a person who works for the government, either at national or local level.

Claim - someone's assertion of their right to something - for example, a claim to the throne.

Conference - a formal meeting to discuss common issues of interest or concern.

Contagious - something that spreads from one person or organism to another, usually referring to illness or disease.

Council - an advisory or administrative body set up to manage the affairs of a place or organisation. The Council of the League of Nations contained the organisation's most powerful members.

Cowpox - a viral disease similar to but much milder than smallpox, transmitted from cows to humans.

Culture - the ideas, customs, and social behaviour of a particular people or society.

D

DNA - the common name for deoxyribonucleic acid, a molecule that contains genetic information and instructions about the development, function and growth of every organism.

Diagnose - to work out the nature or type of a disease, illness or medical condition by looking at the symptoms.

Diagnosis - the identification of a disease, illness or medical condition after considering the symptoms.

Dialysis - the process of cleaning a patient's blood in a machine, removing toxins and excess water, replacing the job of the kidneys.

Diphtheria - a serious bacterial infection that can lead to breathing difficulties, heart failure, paralysis and even death. It mainly affects children.

Dispute - a disagreement or argument; often used to describe conflict between different countries.

Dissection - the careful and methodical cutting apart of a body or plant to inspect its structure.

E

Empire - a group of states or countries ruled over and controlled by a single monarch.

Epidemic - an outbreak of disease that spreads quickly and affects many individuals at the same time.

Eradicate, Eradication - to destroy something and completely wipe it out.

Extreme - furthest from the centre or any given point. If someone holds extreme views, they are not moderate and are considered radical.

F

Fasting - to deliberately refrain from eating, and often drinking, for a period of time.

Fatalities, Fatality - Deaths.

Flagellation - beating or whipping, often done to oneself to show sorrow for sins. In medieval England, it was an attempt to prevent disease.

Front - in war, the area where fighting is taking place.

G

General anaesthetic - a state of controlled unconsciousness using drugs, usually during surgery so the patient can not feel any pain or move.

Genome - the completed DNA set of a human, animal or plant.

Germ - microorganisms that can cause disease. The name was coined by Louis Pasteur as he saw them germinating.

Gong farmer, Gongfermor - a person who removed waste from the streets in Tudor England.

Guild, Guild system - organised groups that controlled different jobs, including apprenticeships and licensing for their specific profession.

H

Hierarchies, Hierarchy - the ranking of people according to authority, for example a colonel in the army being higher than a corporal.

Humanism - a philosophical idea that humans can make up their own minds and ways in the world, rather than being subject to the divine or supernatural.

Hygiene, Hygienic - a term for conditions or practices with the aim of maintaining good health and preventing disease, especially in regard to cleanliness.

I

IVF, In-vitro fertilisation - a method of helping women to become pregnant by fertilising an egg outside the body before returning it to the womb.

Immune, Immune system, Immunity - the body's defence against disease and infection, creating antibodies to fight germs and toxins.

Industrialisation, Industrialise, Industrialised - the process of developing industry in a country or region where previously there was little or none.

Industry - the part of the economy concerned with turning raw materials into into manufactured goods, for example making furniture from wood.

Infection - the result of disease-causing microorganisms finding their way into a wound or suitable body tissue and multiplying.

Inoculation - the introduction of an antigenic substance or vaccine into the body to provide immunity to a specific disease. For example, puss from a smallpox patient was given to an uninfected person, giving them a less severe case of smallpox and future immunity.

L

Laissez-faire - the idea a government should take a hands-off approach to matters such as public health or the free market; it translates from the French as 'let it be'.

Lance, Lanced, Lancing - to prick or cut open something, such as an abscess, and let it drain.

Liberal - politically, someone who believes in allowing personal freedom without too much control by the government or state.

Ligature - something used to tie or bind tightly; an example in medical use is around a limb to slow bleeding from a wound.

Limb - an arm or leg.

Literate - someone who can read and write.

Local anaesthetic - a way to numb an isolated part of the body using medication, for example to prevent pain during minor surgery or stop an injury hurting.

M

Magic bullet - a chemical compound that will kill a specific germ without harming other cells.

Malnutrition - lack of proper nutrition caused by not eating enough of the right things or not having enough to eat. It can also be caused by the body not being able to use the food that is eaten.

Mass - an act of worship in the Catholic Church.

Medieval era, Medieval times, Middle Ages - the period from circa 1250 to 1500.

Miasma, Miasma theory, Miasmata - the theory that diseases were caused by a bad air.

Microbe - a living organism that can only be seen through a microscope.

Minister - a senior member of government, usually responsible for a particular area such as education or finance.

Monasteries, Monastery - a religious building occupied by monks.

Monk - a member of a religious community, often living a simple life of poverty, chastity and work.

Mortality, Mortality rates - refers to death; the mortality rate shows how many people are dying in a society.

N

Neurosurgeon - a surgeon who specialises in neurosurgery.

Neurosurgery - the medical specialism concerned with the diagnosis and treatment of injuries to the brain, spinal cord and spinal column.

P

Peasant - a poor farmer.

Pharmaceutical - relating to medicinal drugs, the industry that manufactures them, and their preparation, use or sale.

Phlegm - the thick liquid produced by the mucous membranes, usually coughed or sneezed out during illness.

Physician - someone qualified to practise medicine, often used as another name for a doctor.

Physiology - the study of how the body works.

Pilgrimage - journey undertaken to a sacred place, usually for religious or spiritual reasons.

Pioneer - the first person to explore or settle in a new area.

Plague - a contagious disease that spreads rapidly.

Pomander - a ball or bag in which to carry pleasant perfumes so that bad smells (miasma) can be avoided.

Population - the number of people who live in a specified place.

Poverty - the state of being extremely poor.

Prevent, Preventative, Preventive - steps taken to stop something from happening.

Printing press - a machine that reproduces writing and images by using ink on paper, making many identical copies.

Proclamation - a public or official announcement of great importance.

Production - a term used to describe how much of something is made, for example saying a factory has a high production rate.

Profit - generally refers to financial gain; the amount of money made after deducting buying, operating or production costs.

Prosthetic, Prosthetic limb - an artificial body part.

Provision - the act of providing or supplying something for someone.

Psychological - referring to a person's mental or emotional state.

Purged, Purging - abrupt and often violent removal of a group of people from a place or organisation; medically, to make someone sick or induce diarrhoea as a treatment to rid them of illness.

Q

Quack - a name for a fake doctor or medical imposter.

Quack cures, Quack remedies - medical treatments that are unscientific so not expected to work.

Quarantine - a period of isolation where a person or animal who has or may have a communicable disease is kept away from others.

R

Rational - when something is based on reason or logic, like science.

Reform, Reforming - change, usually in order to improve an institution or practice.

Regimen sanitatis - a set of instructions on how to maintain good health though a regime.

Relief - something that reduces pressure on people, often through financial or practical support.

Repent, Repented, Repenting - to feel or express remorse and regret for one's wrongdoings or sins.

S

Scrofula - a type of tuberculosis known as "the king's evil" in Europe at one time as it was believed to be cured by royal touch.

Secular - unconnected to religious or spiritual matters; not bound by religious rule.

Sepsis, Septicaemia - life-threatening and potentially fatal blood poisoning, where an existing infection triggers a chain reaction throughout the body.

Shrapnel - small pieces of metal from exploding shells or bombs which caused injuries to soldiers.

Sin - in religion, an immoral act against God's laws.

Skin grafts - a surgical procedure that involves removing healthy skin from one part of the body and transplanting it to a different area.

Smallpox - a contagious and potentially fatal disease that causes high fever, rashes and blisters.

Splint - a strong, straight device used to protect and support a broken limb, keeping it in place.

Spontaneous generation - the theory that rotting material, for example food and excrement, created disease.

State, States - an area of land or a territory ruled by one government.

Sterilisation, Sterilise - to clean something so it is free of bacteria; also refers to a medical procedure that prevents a person from being able to reproduce.

Strike - a refusal by employees to work as a form of protest, usually to bring about change in their working conditions. It puts pressure on their employer, who cannot run the business without workers.

Supernatural - an unscientific explanation for an event or manifestation unattributable to the laws of nature.

Superstition - a firm belief in the supernatural.

Symptom - an indication of something, such as a sign of a

particular illness.

Syphilis - a bacterial infection usually transmitted through sexual contact.

T

Theory of transference, Transference - the theory that you could transfer a disease from a person to something or someone else. An example is the practice of strapping chickens to buboes during the Great Plague.

Transfusion - the process of transferring donated blood to a patient.

V

Vaccination, Vaccine - from the Latin 'vacca', meaning cow. Originally it referred to giving a person cowpox to prevent smallpox, but is now used for all methods of introducing a weak strain of a disease as a way of building immunity.

W

Ward, Wards - A ward is someone who is taken under the protection and power of someone else, usually because it is believed that they do not have the capacity to know what is best for them.

Welfare - wellbeing; often refers to money and services given to the poorest people.

Workhouse - a place for poor people who were unable to work or support themselves.

Y

Yellow bile - pus or stomach acid found in vomit. It was one of the four 'humours' in medieval medicine.

Quizzes, amazing exam preparation tools and more at GCSEHistory.com

Lightning Source UK Ltd.
Milton Keynes UK
UKHW050632160721
387260UK00004B/17